Projects Inspired Architecture

**Rebecca Carnihan
with Julie Ashfield**

Acknowledgements

Rebecca Carnihan would like to thank Executive Headteacher of Grinling Gibbons and Lucas Vale Primary schools, Mrs Cynthia Eubank and the respective Heads of School, Ms Carol Wilson and Ms Tina Harracksingh, all staff and especially the children for their fantastic work for this book. A special thank you is given to Julie Ashfield for her contribution, and to Hilary and Anthony who support my creative endeavours. Thank you.

Julie Ashfield would like to thank Kate Ashfield and the staff and pupils at All Saints C.W Primary Cardiff, St Michaels RC Primary, Pontypridd Rhondda Cynon Taff and St Albans Catholic Primary Cardiff for their fantastic work on the projects in this book.

For Martha and Rosie

Published by Collins
An imprint of HarperCollins*Publishers*
77–85 Fulham Palace Road
Hammersmith
London
W6 8JB

© HarperCollins*Publishers* Limited 2013

10 9 8 7 6 5 4 3 2 1

ISBN-13 978 0 00 746577 4

Rebecca Carnihan and Julie Ashfield assert their moral rights to be identified as the authors of this work.

All rights reserved. No part of this publication may be reproduced, stored in a retrieval system, or transmitted in any form or by any means, electronic, mechanical, photocopying, recording or otherwise, without the prior written permission of the Publisher or a licence permitting restricted copying in the United Kingdom issued by the Copyright Licensing Agency Ltd., 90 Tottenham Court Road, London W1T 4LP.

British Library Cataloguing in Publication Data
A Catalogue record for this publication is available from the British Library

Cover design by Steve Evans Design and Illustration
Internal design by Linda Miles, Lodestone Publishing Limited
Photography by Elmcroft Studios
Edited by Alison Sage and Gaby Frescura
Proofread by Ros and Chris Davies

Printed and bound by Printing Express Limited, Hong Kong

Browse the complete Collins catalogue at
www.collinseducation.com

MIX
Paper from responsible sources
FSC C007454

Contents

Introduction 4

Building with Vision
Floating cities 6
Green homes of the future 7
Monuments in metal 8
Steel and glass structures 9
Beyond the Earth 10
An impression through the window ... 12
Doors to my future 14

Around the World in Ten Buildings
A London panoramic 16
Skyscrapers 17
The Eiffel Tower 18
Life in the Arctic Circle 20
A Berber grain store 21
Gaudi's vision 22
Up on the roof with Gaudi 23
The Taj Mahal 24
Moscow's magical cathedral 25

Community Buildings
Hundertwasser 26
Market day montage 27
My street 28
In the playground 30
A Hindu place of prayer 32
A Christian place of worship 33
The mosque and Islamic architecture 34
A Buddhist temple 35

The Ancient World
Aztec totem statues 36
Ancient Greek columns 37
At home in Benin 38
Benin palace bronzes 39
Pyramid-inspired printmaking 40
Columns for a pharaoh's palace 41
Pyramids brick by brick 42
Chinese houseboats 44
The Great Wall of China 45

Architecture in Stories
A chocolate factory for Charlie 46
Hansel and Gretel gingerbread house 48
Indian tales 49
The old woman who lived in a shoe .. 50
Tightrope between the towers 51
At Home with The Twits 52
Narnia and eternal winter 53

Building Britain
Gladiators at the amphitheatre 54
Wattle and daub settlements 56
Tower of London hats 57
Tudor timber-framed houses 58
A Victorian school building 60
Foggy smoggy top hats 61
Inside a Victorian factory 62
Victorian factory looms 63
The Blitz: sheltering underground 64
The Blitz: a city in ruins 65

Getting from A to B
Brunel's bridges 66
Bridges for this millennium 67
Roman arches 68
Arches in viaducts 69
Tunnel vision 70
A panorama of our school 71
Visiting heritage houses 72

Introduction

This book contains a wide range of art activities and display ideas inspired by architecture throughout the world and across time. There are seven chapters covering different aspects of architecture.

There is scope for children to contribute to and innovate within the projects, adding characters, speech bubbles, scenery and a narrative. You will find the children's contribution to a project's development leads to a valuable and stimulating exchange of ideas, and can be a springboard for work in other disciplines such as literacy, drama, history, geography and science.

Each project begins with a whole-class introduction, usually with stimulating material from the internet and other sources, followed by a practical activity, which might include drawing, painting, printing, 3D modelling or sculpture, as well as wearable art.

Chapter 1: Building with Vision

Explore the imaginary side of architecture, looking at futuristic-looking buildings, imagining buildings in unusual places such as afloat on the ocean or on the Moon.

Chapter 2: Around the World in Ten Buildings

This chapter takes you on a journey to different geographical locations to visit famous buildings and monuments, and also examines innovative buildings that use local resources, or have outstanding artistic elements.

Chapter 3: Community Buildings

This chapter focuses on local buildings close to where you live, or that are used by the community. There is an opportunity to make sketches out and about, look at local geography, and think about how you might like to use your own ideas to improve what is around you.

Chapter 4: The Ancient World

Go back in time to some of the world's great civilizations and explore the architectural designs that were used in palaces, places of prayer and power, as well as ordinary homes. The projects are based on popular history projects studied by classes in primary schools.

Chapter 5: Architecture in Stories

In this chapter, creating buildings from stories will enrich children's literacy experience and will help them to visualise an unfolding tale. Here there is also the opportunity to develop characters and speech bubbles to animate the work.

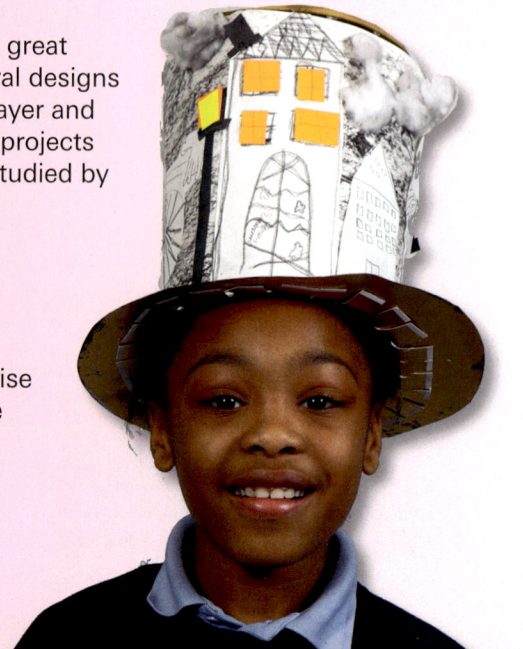

Introduction

Chapter 6: Building Britain

Go back in time and look at significant buildings which have played a part in Britain's history. Many of the buildings reflect their social history, for example, the factories of the Industrial Revolution.

Chapter 7: Getting from A to B

Although it may not always be obvious, getting from A to B is helped a great deal by architecture. This chapter shows the importance of bridges and tunnels in everyday use and looks at the variation and ambition behind projects such as the work of Brunel. See how the simple arch has contributed to engineering since the time of the Romans and make design and technology links by building your own arches.

Adapting projects for older and younger readers

The projects that have been photographed for this book were largely carried out by KS2 children. However, the ideas could easily be adapted and simplified for younger children, who will still be able to produce some inspiring outcomes. The aim for these art activities is to deepen the children's understanding of the local environment, history and geography and to develop their skills in spatial awareness and design.

Skills and techniques

There are a wide variety of media and techniques, with 2D and 3D work throughout the book. Many projects use core resources, including: Modroc, PVA glue, paper straws, pipe cleaners, poster paints, black sugar paper, cartridge paper, coloured paper or card and cardboard boxes (it is useful to collect, flatten and store these after school deliveries).

It is a good idea to build up a box of resources, materials and clean recyclables that have interesting textures such as string, wool, sandpaper, fabric scraps, twigs, buttons, bottle lids, lolly sticks, cotton wool, sponges, paper art straws and raffia. These can be used to make impressions or can be incorporated into a finished artwork.

For interesting resources and materials, find out if there is a children's scrap project in your local area. They are usually charitable organisations that gather clean waste from manufacturers specifically for schools and youth groups. Alternatively, contact your local council for information about similar schemes.

I hope that these activities prove exciting and bring out the best in your children!

Rebecca Carnihan

Building with Vision

Floating cities

Start by asking children: *'If building on land becomes difficult in the future, how would you design a city on the sea?'* Older children will enjoy exploring ideas around survival, science and technology, as well as environmental issues. Look at examples from science fiction, images of architects' unrealised visions for the future on the internet, and the Eden Project in Cornwall. Discuss what resources would be needed, for example, fresh water, sustainable food sources, a place to live. Ask children to draw their idea of a floating city and to list the materials they will use before starting to build it.

Resources
- Polystyrene
- Cutting knife (adult use only)
- Recyclable materials such as plastic water bottles and lids, lolly sticks, pipe cleaners, headless matchsticks
- Tissue paper
- PVA glue

Model-making

Approach

1. There are many possibilities for making floating living spaces, so encourage each child's imaginative ideas. Ask children to choose a flat piece of polystyrene that has been cut or broken into shape by an adult. An idea for a floating living space is listed below.
   - Make a greenhouse for leisure or for growing food, from the side of a plastic bottle that has been cut in half by an adult, then filled with tissue paper.
   - Make a living area by using the top of a plastic bottle to form a dome and provide protection from the Sun.
   - Make fences, trees and flowers using lolly sticks, pipe cleaners and matchsticks.
2. Ask children to push all these materials into the polystyrene. First dip the materials in PVA glue, to keep them in place.

Cross-curricular links

Geography: investigate how rising sea levels are impacting on the world.
Literacy: write a fantasy story about life in a floating city of the future.
Science: research water and why it is important for life.

Building with Vision

Green homes of the future

In this project, children can investigate recycling and make a clay model of a community from the future. Children can use parts from an old computer to reflect the high-tech aspects of their community.

Drawing, map-making and 3D clay modelling

Approach

1. Using images from the internet, discuss with children what a community needs to be sustainable. Before they make the clay models, ask them to make drawings and maps of imaginary island communities.

2. Cover the working surface with newspaper and guide children in using a rolling pin and clay grids to roll out a lump of clay. To make a circular clay base, they should only use a clay board, turning the board regularly as they roll the clay. Once this is done, trim the clay into a circle using a small plate as a template. Encourage children to use damp sponges to wipe away excess clay as they work.

3. Demonstrate how to make spheres, cylinders, cubes and cuboids. Gently roll a lump of clay to make a sphere; tap a sphere on the board to flatten the sides and make a cube.

4. Mix clay and water to the consistency of single cream to make slip. Score the bottom of the 3D shapes before fixing them firmly with slip to the clay base. Cover the clay model with a plastic bag to keep it moist between sessions.

5. Discuss adding computer parts and any other details, and allow the models to dry. Paint the models with a protective varnish made up of a mixture of half PVA glue and half water before displaying all the children's work, including the drawings, maps, plans and photographs.

Resources
- Images of various communities taken from the internet
- A3 paper for maps and drawings
- Marker pens
- Newspaper
- Rolling pins and clay grids
- Air-drying clay
- Clay board and modelling tools
- Small plates
- Damp sponges
- Water (to make slip)
- Plastic bags
- Computer parts (adult help)
- PVA glue and water mixture
- Paintbrushes

Cross-curricular links

Geography: research the type of land that would provide a sustainable lifestyle. Where in the world might it be best?
Science: research different types of green homes and discuss their special features.

Monuments in metal

This project is inspired by buildings made of metal. One of the most famous ones is the Sydney Opera House in Australia, which inspired the Thames Barrier in London. More recently, architect Frank Gehry who has designed music venues and museums worldwide, has made buildings of aluminium and other lightweight and flexible metals. Gehry manipulates simple shapes, sometimes using twisted soda cans to create a model of a building through folding and layering.

Resources
- Scissors
- Scrap paper
- Cardboard box
- Poster paints and brushes
- Silver paper
- PVA glue
- Paper clips
- Pipe cleaners and additional drawings (optional)

Model buildings

Approach

1. Start with an exercise in improvisation. Ask children to cut out a simple shape from scrap paper in different sizes. Then get them to bend and fold the cut-outs to make new shapes and forms, for example, squares, circles or hexagons.

2. Prepare a base for the model. The cardboard box will become the model platform. Paint the outside green if the building will be near green space or paint it blue if it will be near a river. Add traffic if it will be in an urban environment.

3. Using the silver paper, begin to construct the building. Think about the interior and exterior such as adding a staircase and windows. Children may need help with this. Glue the pieces in position with a little PVA glue, holding them together temporarily with paper clips. Once dry, remove the paper clips carefully.

4. Suggest that children make small standing figures using pipe cleaners. They can also draw features, such as a car park, onto paper and stick them on.

Cross-curricular links

Literacy: use information texts to research Frank Gehry's work and write a report about it.
Maths: investigate the properties of 3D shapes.
Science: research the properties of metals used in building construction.

Building with Vision

Steel and glass structures

Some of the world's most amazing buildings have inspired this project, which is suitable for older children to research by themselves. Children can then make imaginative wire structures, which they can cover with collage made with mixed media.

Wire creations

Approach

1. Introduce the project with an internet presentation of images of the Gherkin and the Shard in London, and Crystal Towers in Dubai. Do children see any similarities? Ask them to draw the parts of the buildings that they like best. Make a display of the children's drawings. They could also make a 'word wall' of vocabulary to describe the buildings.

2. Under careful supervision, ask children to experiment with different ways of shaping and bending wire. In small groups, use small pieces of masking tape to bandage together two pieces of wire to make an abstract building. To extend the building, bandage a new piece of wire parallel to the existing structure and bend the wire upwards.

3. When the skeleton building is complete, carefully add a 'skin' of plastic food wrap around the frame.

4. Place the wire structures on a pile of newspaper to absorb the drips of water. Supply each group with a shallow tub of water and a supply of pieces of brown tape. Dip a piece of brown tape (sticky side down) in the water. Shake off the excess water and smooth the tape onto the plastic food wrap layer so that each piece of tape overlaps the next. Cover the entire frame and leave until dry.

5. Encourage children to draw on their models and make collages with cut up photocopies of their drawings and architectural drawings and PVA glue.

Resources

- Internet images of the Gherkin, the Shard and Crystal Towers
- A3 paper
- Marker pens
- Wire that is easy to bend, cut into 1 m lengths
- Masking tape, pre-cut
- Plastic food wrap
- Newspaper
- Shallow tubs filled with water
- Brown paper tape cut into 3 cm pieces
- Architectural drawings, photocopied to A4 size
- PVA glue

Cross-curricular links

Literacy: write a description of a popular modern building and explain why it might be so well liked. Various buildings have names such as the 'Gherkin'. Think of names for three buildings in the neighbourhood.

Beyond the Earth

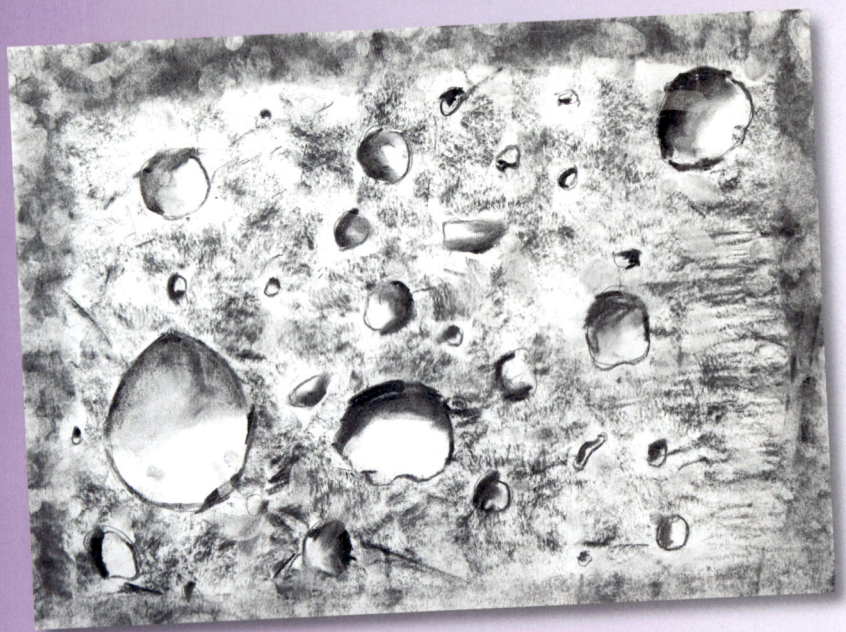

Start by asking children what they think it would be like to live on the Moon. This project explores our nearest neighbour in space through drawings of the surface of the Moon made by using charcoal to show the sharp contrast of light and dark. Show children the stunning images taken by the astronauts during the *Apollo* space missions, so that they can see the extreme contrasts, especially in and around the Moon's craters.

Charcoal drawings

Approach

1. To make moon drawings, get children to first practise using charcoal on scrap paper. Use the charcoal sticks on their sides, dragging them across the paper and smudging some areas with fingertips. Press hard or lightly for a range of marks and shades. Work back into the smudged areas with darker lines, or make lighter patches by rubbing with fingers or a rubber.

2. For the Moon surface, draw several craters of different sizes on cartridge paper. Using the techniques explored in Step 1, create contrasting dark and light areas in and around each crater.

3. Spray with fixative or hairspray outside to minimise smudging.

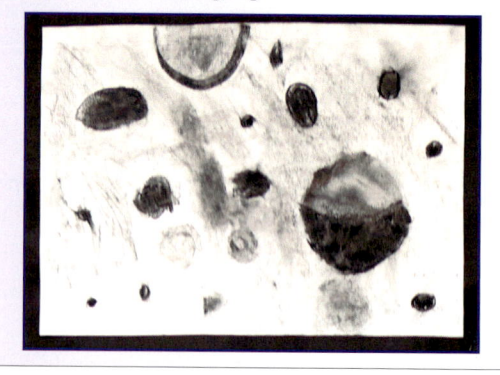

Resources
- Moon drawings
- Fine charcoal sticks
- Scrap paper
- A2 cartridge paper
- Rubbers
- Fixative or hairspray (adult use only)
- Moon models
- Newspaper or newsprint
- Cardboard, 1 m × 1 m or smaller
- Masking tape
- Modroc
- PVA glue and water
- Black and white paint
- Paintbrushes
- Silver glitter
- Silver paper

Building with Vision

Modroc models

Approach

1. Discuss the idea of living on the Moon and building a Moonbase. Points could include the effects of lack of gravity, lack of oxygen, producing food, shielding people from the Sun, transport across the Moon and travelling back and forth to Earth.

2. Each child can make a crater. Twist thin strips of newspaper or newsprint, bend it into a circle and tape it to the cardboard base with masking tape. Using Modroc (see page 22), layer a few pieces over the paper crater, smoothing it as you go. Cover with two layers if necessary.

3. Thin some PVA glue with a little water and brush onto the dry powdery plaster surface to seal it.

4. Mix black and white paint to make dark grey and use it to paint a curve across the cardboard base, filling in this section to show the dark side of the Moon. Add more white paint to make light grey and use it to paint the light side of the Moon. The craters should be slightly lighter than the surrounds and black in the centre.

5. On the light side of the Moon, brush PVA glue on some craters' edges and sprinkle with silver glitter to add shine.

6. Make dome-shaped buildings for the Moonbase using circles of silver paper folded into different shapes.

7. Brush the edge of each shape with PVA glue and position on the Moon's surface.

Cross-curricular links

Literacy: keep a Moon journal about what it would be like to live on a Moonbase.

Science: investigate why the Moon appears different to us from day to day. Do some research on light and shadow.

An impression through the window

This project is inspired by well-known landscape paintings by the Impressionists. When designing buildings and deciding where to position windows, architects often consider how to make the most of views of the surrounding landscapes from inside the building.

Allow children to explore colour mixing. Examples of colour-rich Impressionist paintings are Monet's *Water Lilies* series, Van Gogh's *Cypress Trees* series and Cezanne's paintings in Provence, France.

Resources
- A3 colour images of chosen paintings
- A3 cartridge paper
- Drawing pencils
- Acrylic or poster paints and brushes
- Scissors
- White flexible card
- PVA glue and sticky tape

Framed landscapes

Approach

1. Provide a selection of A3 colour copies of Impressionist landscapes for the children to look at and talk about. Encourage them to choose a painting and place it alongside a sheet of cartridge paper and before drawing anything, to look carefully at it. *Is there a horizon line? Is it halfway up or two-thirds down the picture?* Then ask them to draw the picture. *What overall shapes can be seen?* Ask them to draw these in lightly. Persuade children to ignore 'mistakes' and keep going.

2. Practise colour mixing and encourage children to begin to paint in the areas of green that they can see in the Impressionist painting. A good exercise is to use the double-primary palette system, which uses eight colours:
   - red, blue and yellow in a warm range
   - red, blue and yellow in a cool range
   - black and white.

Building with Vision

3   Children can mix warm and cool blues and yellows to produce different shades of green. Once they find a match in the painting for a particular green, they should use it. Ready-mixed greens produce less accurate shades.

4   Encourage children to use this mixing process for each colour. As the colours build up, they can try to copy the kind of brush strokes the artist used. Van Gogh built up colour using dash marks, while Monet blended his colours.

5   Make removable window frames for the display. Cut strips of card the same size as the four sides of the picture and use PVA glue to stick them together. Attach one side of the frame to the back of the painting with sticky tape, on one edge only, to be able to peel back the frame.

Cross-curricular links

Art: research the colour wheel and experiment with colour mixing.
Geography: choose four Impressionist paintings and research the places where they were painted.
History: research the lives of the Impressionists.
Literacy: write a diary entry of a famous painter as he or she worked on a masterpiece.
Science: use a prism to split 'white' light. How do we see colour? Research light and dark.

Doors to my future

This project aims to help children explore the idea of building their future. What would children like to do or be in adult life? Ask the children to imagine their future as a building and visualise the door into the building. What do they hope to see when they walk through the door? Start a discussion where everyone voices their ambitions. Tell children that they needn't limit themselves to one aspiration and will not be judged on how realistic it is. For example, someone may want to be a doctor and/or a top footballer; the more ideas the better. Also discuss hobbies and clubs, and what they like to do now, both in school and during their own time. Work towards a reflective piece about the here and now, as well as what could be.

Resources
- A2 flexible card
- Crayons
- A4 colour paper
- A3 white paper
- PVA glue
- A4, A3 prints of photographs of children from behind
- Scissors
- Black writing pens
- Glitter (optional)

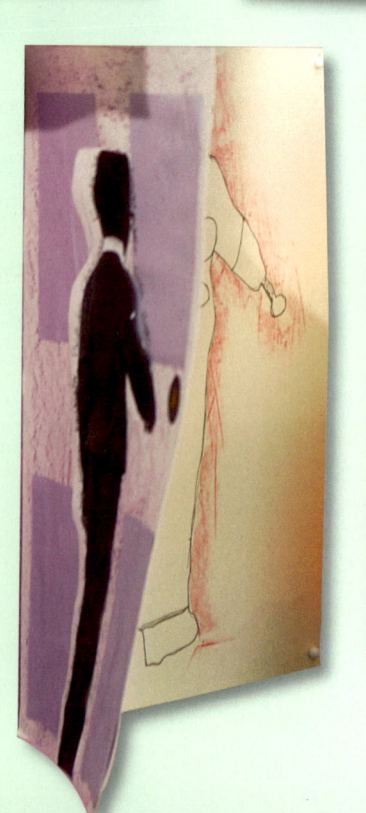

Building with Vision

3D cut-outs

Approach

1. Fold an A2 sheet of card in half and rub the side of a crayon over the front cover. Then take an A4 sheet of colour paper, the same colour as the crayon, fold twice and cut along the folds to make four rectangles. Glue onto the card, leaving a 2–3 cm gap between each rectangle so that it resembles panels on a door.

2. Encourage children to cut out their large and small prints. Ask them to draw around the large figure onto A3 white paper and cut it out to make a white silhouette.

3. Open the folded card and draw around the silhouette figure repeatedly from left to right. Using the black writing pen, ask children to draw themselves as the different people they might like to be in the future, adding a sentence or collection of words around the edge of each figure about those aspirations. Get them to skim the outside edge of each figure using the side of a crayon.

4. Ask children to select two or three cut-out figures and arrange on the front of the 'door'. When they are happy with the layout, children should stick down the figures with PVA glue. Get them to glue on a small black circle as the door knob the figure is reaching for. Add glitter for a magical effect.

5. Encourage children to write words or sentences around the figure on the front cover as before, this time describing their feelings about and hopes for the future.

Cross-curricular links

Literacy: write an account of the first day in a dream job and the first day in an unpleasant job.
Maths: work out the perimeters and areas of doors around the school and look at the height and width of standard doors.
Science: imagine being a scientist in the future. What would they be working on?

Around the World in Ten Buildings

A London panoramic

The city of London is the focus for this project, but it can be adapted to reflect any town or city. Encourage children to look closely at landmarks and buildings, focusing on their overall shape, use of glass or patterns of brickwork. *Are they modern or old?* Explore ways to describe the skyline in words. If a class trip is possible, children can write about the atmosphere on the streets and the sights they have seen. Using black, white and all the shades of grey, children can create a strong, large-scale piece of work. They can also explore light and dark as well as the use of silhouettes.

Collage

Approach

1. To make the buildings, ask children to choose an A3 sheet of black paper or white paper and draw buildings with black or white pastels.
2. Use strips of paper to create the lines of the buildings.
3. Cut out letters or words from newspapers and the sheet of words the children created, which they feel describe the buildings and where they are. Use PVA glue to stick the letters and words on the collage, making them part of the buildings.
4. Cut out the buildings just outside the lines.
5. To make the background, mix a pale shade of grey from the black and white paint. Using sponge pieces, apply paint in blocks on the large roll of plain paper or wallpaper, to create silhouettes of towers.
6. Repeat the process further down the paper, with a darker shade of grey. Finally, they can add some white silhouettes.
7. Position and stick buildings onto the bottom of the skyline with PVA glue.

Resources
- Black A3 sugar paper or white A3 paper
- Black and white oil pastels
- Strips of paper
- Scissors
- Newspapers and sheet of words and alphabet
- PVA glue
- Black and white poster paint
- Sponges cut into 2 cm × 2 cm pieces
- Large roll of plain paper or wallpaper

Cross-curricular links

Geography: examine the development of your town or city. Where did it start?
History: imagine walking through London 100 years ago. What would it have been like?
Literacy: describe walking or travelling through your neighbourhood.

Around the World in Ten Buildings

Skyscrapers

By the 20th century, the race for the tallest building in the world had begun. Would it be the Chrysler building or the Bank of Manhattan? Chrysler architects added a thin spire at the last minute to snatch the prize. Which building would win the competition today? In this project, children can investigate skyscrapers and then design their own.

Designing tall structures

Approach

1. Show children images of the tallest skyscrapers in the world. Discuss the buildings and invite children to create their own imaginative skyscrapers, while working collaboratively in small groups.

2. Explain to children that each group will share a large sheet of paper and that each child will draw their own section of skyscraper. Discuss the importance of planning. *Who will do what?*

3. Give each group an A1 sheet and drawing materials. When the group pictures are underway, tell children to stop and look at one another's work.

4. Discuss the colours that children wish to use. In the example in the photograph, the class chose a colour palette of reds and oranges.

5. Cut out each individual section and glue on to card, building up a whole skyscraper. Leaving a narrow border, cut out the whole building. Staple skyscrapers to the display, showing their different heights. Children should add their own labels to explain any important details.

6. Imitate the Chrysler building architects and add a 'spire' made of pipe cleaners.

Resources
- Images of skyscrapers
- Sheets of A1 paper
- Marker pens
- Oil pastels
- Scissors
- PVA glue
- Coloured card
- Stapler (adult use only)
- Pipe cleaners

Cross-curricular links

Geography: make a map showing the ten tallest buildings in the world.

History: investigate the history of the elevator, which made the use of skyscrapers feasible.

Maths: find out and compare the heights of some of the world's tallest buildings.

The Eiffel Tower

This famous French architectural icon was built by Gustave Eiffel in 1889. The instantly recognisable image works well to use as part of French studies and in projects on Victorian engineering. The group display should be big and bold and resemble a Cubist painting. The process has an element of mystery because each child works on a separate piece, which is recognisable only once the display is assembled. Children can also make individual towers on smaller panels.

3D construction and Cubist display

Approach

1. To make individual towers, cut rectangular panels of cardboard slightly narrower than A4. Demonstrate to children how to sketch a version of the Eiffel Tower onto cardboard, guiding them where to draw a line for the top, stage two, stage one and the base of the tower.

2. With PVA glue, stick matchsticks onto the drawing, building up as much detail as possible.

3. Tear off a generous piece of foil, bigger than the panel. Spread PVA glue over the entire panel, and starting at the centre, place the foil on top so that it is overlapping on all sides like a border.

4. Starting at the centre of the piece, carefully press the foil over and around the matchsticks, to make a relief of the construction underneath. Do this before folding the edges of the foil around the back, otherwise it will tear. Glue the edges to the back of the cardboard.

5. Mix together black and brown paint to make a very dark brown. Paint over the panel and before it dries, wipe away the paint from the raised parts with a small dry sponge. Use tissues to remove the last bits of paint.

Resources
- Scissors
- Cardboard
- PVA glue
- Headless matchsticks
- Strong aluminium foil
- Black and brown paint
- Paintbrushes
- Small sponges
- Tissues
- Photocopied images of the Eiffel Tower
- Plastic or paper straws

Around the World in Ten Buildings

6   To make a group tower, enlarge a picture of the Eiffel Tower using a photocopier, and cut it into rectangles. Cut rectangular pieces of cardboard suitable for each section of the tower. Hand out a cardboard rectangle to each child, together with a section of the Eiffel Tower picture and repeat Steps 2 to 5. Ask children to copy the picture onto their piece of cardboard and create a 3D construction on it with straws.

7   To assemble, pin each panel to a display board, overlapping where necessary to form a large and different Eiffel Tower.

Cross-curricular links

Art: look at Cubism in Paris in the early 20th century.
Geography: research a project on Paris.
History: research 19th century architects around the world. Look at the big 19th century World Fairs.
Literacy: write an imaginary diary from the point of view of a workman who helped to construct the Eiffel Tower.

Life in the Arctic Circle

With children, look at and discuss Inuit culture and how people live in the extreme temperatures of the Arctic. In this project, models are built to show the inside and outside of an igloo. In the display, the fascinating phenomenon of the Northern Lights (*Aurora Borealis*) is visible in the skies above the igloo, represented using coloured fabric. These swirls of coloured light in the *Aurora Borealis* are the result of geomagnetic storms high in the atmosphere.

Resources
- Scissors
- Cardboard
- PVA glue
- A shallow cardboard or shoebox
- White and black poster paint
- Paintbrushes
- White paper
- Coloured pencils
- Net fabric in fluorescent colours
- Glue gun (adult use only)

Model-making

Approach

1. To make the igloo, cut some cardboard squares, about 5 cm × 5 cm. Glue them on a box lid with PVA glue to build up an igloo-brick effect.

2. Once the glue is dry, paint the outside of the box with two to three coats of white acrylic paint. Once the paint is dry, paint the interior of the box black.

3. Cut out small squares of white paper and glue them inside the box in a semi-circle to make the rooftop of the igloo.

4. Draw and colour in pictures for the interior, showing animal skins, drying fish, snow shoes and beds made of ice. Cut out and stick them inside the igloo. Add two people outside pointing up to the sky.

5. To make the Northern Lights, cut strips of net fabric, arrange them and attach them to the box with a glue gun.

Cross-curricular links

Geography: research climate change and the shrinking of the Arctic ice caps. What does this mean for animals that live there? Research animal habitats and adaptation.

Literacy: write a description of life in the Arctic winter from an Inuit point of view.

Science: investigate why the Arctic is called the 'Land of the Midnight Sun'.

Around the World in Ten Buildings

A Berber grain store

Introduce children to the Berber-grain stores, which were built in Tunisia in the 13th century by the Berbers to protect the grain from the heat and to protect the settlement from invaders. This project takes a look at North Africa and links in well to studies on Egypt. Traditional colours worn by Berber people are fuchsia, red, brown and sky blue. The Berber stores were used in the *Star Wars* films, so film and science fiction fans can adapt the project by adding a droid or two.

Resources
- Drawing pencils
- Cardboard, A4 size
- Newspaper or newsprint
- Masking tape
- Modroc and water
- PVA glue and water mixture
- Poster paint and brushes
- Dry sand
- Pipe cleaners
- Lolly sticks
- Card
- Scissors
- Felt

3D Modroc sculptures

Approach

1. To make the grain stores, ask the children to draw the outline of a grain store on a piece of cardboard. They can twist thin strips of newspaper, bend them and tape them to the outline.

2. Have children layer Modroc (see page 22) piece by piece over the paper structure, smoothing it down as they go. Cover the structure with two layers. The surface will be uneven and bumpy but that is the aim.

3. Thin some PVA glue with a little water and brush onto the dry plaster to seal the powdery surface. Mix a very light sandy colour with poster paint and a little PVA glue and paint onto the dry surface. While this paint is still wet, sprinkle on some dry sand.

4. To make Berber people, wrap a pipe cleaner around a lolly stick to make arms. Colour the card and cut out a small piece of card for the face. Glue this at the top of the lolly stick. Cut two brightly-coloured pieces of felt to form the front and back of the robe. Cut a strip of felt for a headscarf, layering it with PVA glue and wrapping it around the head. Add vertical stripes to the robe for more colour. Add generous amounts of PVA to the back of each figure and position on the grain store.

Cross-curricular links

Geography: Berbers are semi-nomadic. Research nomadic peoples and find out what kind of dwellings they live in.

Gaudi's vision

Introduce children to the colourful work of Antoni Gaudi, the eccentric 19th century Catalan architect who helped to make Barcelona one of Europe's most exciting cities. Gaudi was interested in nature and rarely used straight lines, so investigate the organic themes in his work. Point out how the balconies and windows of his buildings are all curved, irregular and playful. This project is based on details from Casa Milà, Casa Batlló and Park Güell. It is a great starting point for making free-form shapes.

Resources
- Scissors
- Cardboard off-cuts
- Masking tape
- Newspaper or newsprint
- Plastic straws
- Modroc and water
- PVA glue and water
- Brushes
- Coloured tissue paper

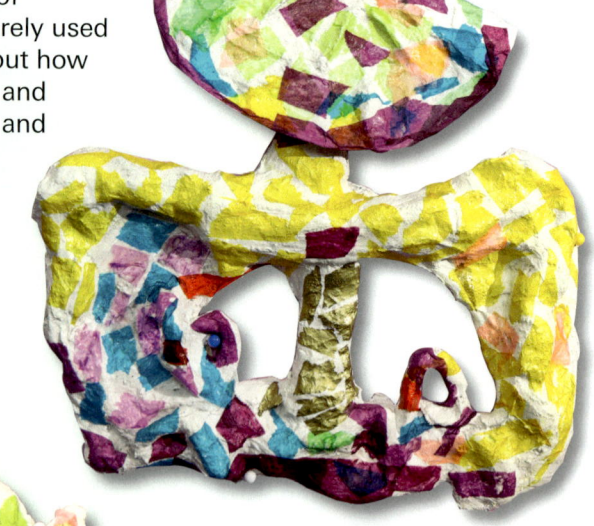

Modroc sculptures

Approach

1. Cut a pile of cardboard pieces at different angles and curves for children to choose from.
2. Encourage them to take several pieces to form a four-sided shape, and tape the pieces together.
3. To make the structures, ask children to use newspaper or newsprint, and tear, twist or scrunch the pieces and tape them to create the curved forms of Gaudi's balconies and windows. To achieve the skeletal forms on the balconies of Casa Batlló, add plastic straws across the opening of the cardboard frame.
4. Cut a pile of Modroc strips 3–4 cm wide (one roll between two is a good start). Show children how to use Modroc by dipping it in water once and allowing excess water to run off. Massage it to soften and place each piece in turn over the structure until it is entirely covered. Allow at least a day to set hard.
5. Encourage children to look at Gaudi's fantastic mosaics. Demonstrate how to brush the model with watered-down PVA glue, covering a small area at a time. Stick on pieces of cut or torn tissue paper to add spectacular colour and brush on an additional layer of the PVA mixture for a shiny gloss finish.

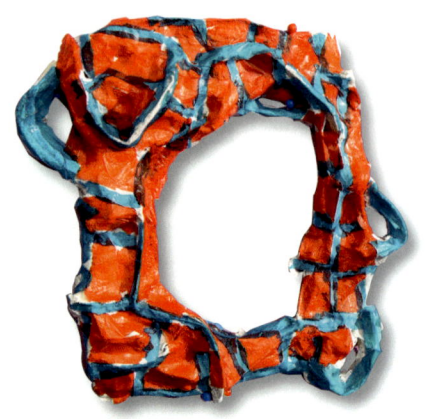

Cross-curricular links

Design and Technology: try to make a building with organic shapes without using straight lines.
Geography: write a report on how the city of Barcelona has grown and developed over the last century.
Literacy: research the life of Antoni Gaudi.

Around the World in Ten Buildings

Up on the roof with Gaudi

This project celebrates Antoni Gaudi's wonderfully colourful work. Start by showing children images of the rooftops of Casa Milà and Casa Batlló. Look closely at the patterns in Gaudi's mosaics in Park Güell. He used many different materials such as broken china, broken bottles and tiles to create an explosion of colour.

Resources
- Scissors
- Small paper plates
- Stapler (adult use only)
- Newspaper or newsprint
- Masking tape
- Plastic straws
- Modroc and water
- Flexible card
- Coloured tissue paper
- PVA glue and water
- Glue gun (adult use only)
- Brushes

Mosaic chimneys

Approach

1. Show children how to cut into the centre of a paper plate and overlap to create a cone shape. Staple it into position.
2. Ask children to tear, twist or scrunch pieces of newsprint and tape them on to create a unique chimney that perhaps has a spiral bumps.
3. Children should use Modroc (see page opposite) to cover the paper structure, including up and under the edges. Allow to set hard.
4. To make the chimney stack, roll the flexible card into a tube and staple to secure.
5. Cut or tear a mixture of tissue papers to add spectacular colour, both to the chimney top and stack. Use PVA glue thinned with a little water to stick. Brush on an additional layer of PVA mixture to give a shiny gloss finish.
6. Add PVA glue to the stack, place the cone on top and leave to bond. Or use a glue gun to speed up the process.

Cross-curricular links

Art: make a mosaic.
History: research the lives of the child chimney sweeps.
Literacy: write the story of a young chimney sweep.
Science: research the causes of air pollution. What can be done about it?

23

The Taj Mahal

Show children images of the Taj Mahal, built by Mughal Emperor Shah Jahan in memory of his wife. One of the Seven Wonders of the World, the Taj Mahal is a beautiful example of Islamic architecture. At dawn and sunset, its white marble takes on a glorious pink glow. This project involves clay modelling, carving, mixing plaster and casting. The casting process provides a good science link as it demonstrates how a liquid turns into a solid.

Plaster casts

Approach

1. To begin modelling and carving, cover surfaces with plastic sheeting and use the rolling pin to roll out the clay to form a slab, about 25 cm wide × 15 cm long × 4 cm deep.

2. Using their fingers and thumbs, ask children to pinch the edges of the clay to build up a thick wall 2–3 cm high. Check for cracks and use extra clay to patch as necessary.

3. Encourage children to smooth the clay within the wall and use the modelling tools to draw a simplified version of the Taj Mahal. To make the three rooftop domes, ask children to scoop out hollows in the clay with a tool and smooth with their fingers. To make the arches below, add triangular pieces of clay in a row. (Everything will come out the opposite way once cast.)

4. Children can do plaster casting with careful supervision. Pour two cups of water into a plastic container, stir in two tablespoons of PVA glue and sprinkle one cup (or more) of plaster of Paris into the water without stirring. When the plaster forms a peak out of the water, stir gently with a spoon until the mixture looks like thick cream.

5. Add a squirt of bright pink paint and fold in gently to keep the marbled effect.

6. Pour the plaster quickly into the clay mould and smooth over with the back of a tablespoon. Allow to set for at least a day before peeling off the clay carefully (the clay can be kept moist and used again). Clean off small bits of damp clay with a toothpick and wash the plaster cast under running water. Allow to dry.

Resources
- Equipment for clay work
- Plastic sheets to protect surfaces
- Rolling pins and clay grids
- Clay
- Modelling tools
- Water
- Plastic containers
- Measuring cups and spoons
- PVA glue
- Plaster of Paris
- Pink poster paint and brushes
- Toothpicks

Cross-curricular links

History: research the Mughals and Shah Jahan.

Literacy: write a journal of one of the artists working on the Taj Mahal. Intended as 'a vision of heaven', how was it built?

Science: investigate the different states of materials. How can a liquid turn into a solid?

Around the World in Ten Buildings

Moscow's magical cathedral

St Basil's Cathedral in Moscow was built by Ivan the Terrible. Show children images of its distinctive onion-shaped roofs, candy colours and gingerbread appearance and have fun creating rooftop designs in different patterns and colour combinations.

Cathedral collages

Approach

1. Encourage children to draw an onion-shaped template on a piece of flexible card and draw around it several times in rows on the cartridge paper. These will become the distinctive tower tops of the cathedral.

2. Ask children to draw a different pattern on each one. This is an opportunity for them to create their own designs. Paint each shape with exciting colours.

3. Cut three to five strips of brown or orange paper in varying widths and heights. Draw the cathedral's brick pattern onto each one. Arrange the towers on the sheet of black paper at different heights and stick them on with glue.

4. Cut around each onion shape and glue into position at the top of each tower. Dab a little glue and sprinkle on some gold glitter.

5. Once dry, cut around the pictures leaving an edge of about 1 cm, then mount onto blue backing paper. The shade of blue you choose will affect whether the cathedral appears on a sunny day or a wintry day.

Resources
- Drawing pencils
- Flexible card
- A4 cartridge paper
- Paint and brushes
- Scissors
- Brown or orange paper
- A3 black sugar paper
- Glue sticks
- Gold glitter
- Blue backing paper

Cross-curricular links

Geography: research the conditions of a Russian winter.
History: write a report about Ivan the Terrible. Why was he given this name?
RE: write a report about Russian churches and religious rituals.

Community Buildings

Hundertwasser

Talk about Friedensreich Hundertwasser, who was born in Austria and was active in the 1950s. He was influenced a lot by fellow Austrian artist Gustav Klimt. Show children examples of the detailed, decorative and colourful paintings by both artists. Hundertwasser transferred his approach into architecture, creating colourful and fun places to live. Have a discussion and find words to describe his buildings, for example, *colourful, curvy, fun, fancy, elaborate*.

Resources
- Cardboard rectangles and scraps
- Cardboard panels A4 to A3 size
- Scissors
- PVA glue
- Paper art straws
- White and acrylic paints or coloured poster paints with PVA
- Paintbrushes

Cardboard collage

Approach

1. Gather a selection of cardboard rectangles and scraps and begin to assemble them onto a cardboard panel to build the façade of one of Hundertwasser's blocks of flats.

2. Once they are happy with the way the pieces are arranged, have them stick the pieces down with PVA glue, adding small squares of card for windows, and art straws for any vertical or horizontal lines. Bend the straws to form curves.

3. Paint the entire surface white. Once completely dry, add colour with a fine paintbrush. Use colours such as yellow, red, blue or black, as Hundertwasser did.

Cross-curricular links

Geography: research homes for a hot climate and for a cold climate.

Literacy: describe your ideal home. Write a play about someone who builds a house completely different from any in the neighbourhood.

Community Buildings

Market day montage

Take a trip to your local market or high street as part of a project to investigate your local area. For this project, children should take photographs and write lists of what they see, hear, smell and experience. Back in the classroom, use this research to create an atmospheric scene of the locality, by combining line drawing and photography.

Resources
- Digital camera
- A3 prints of digital photos
- Glue sticks
- A3 cartridge paper
- Black writing pens

Mixed media montage

Approach

1. Print the pictures that children took during their visit to the local market in A3 size, in black and white.

2. Ask children to choose a print and fold it horizontally in half. Cut along the fold. Then glue the top half of the picture to the cartridge paper.

3. Keep the lower half of the picture nearby and look at the details in that half of the picture. Instruct children to begin to draw the detail they see onto the blank half of the cartridge paper, for example, adding people's legs or the lower half of a building. Ask them to draw as much detail as possible.

Cross-curricular links

Geography: draw a map of the local market with a key for the different stalls, and anything else that was there.

History: research the history of your local area.

Literacy: write a poem about the local market, concentrating on the sounds, sights, colours, smells, feelings and other things that the scene brings to mind.

27

My street

Start by asking children: *Do you live in a house or in a flat? Are the windows big or small?* Encourage children to draw their own house or to sketch buildings in their area.

The children's models pictured here are of tower blocks in an urban environment. This project is based on artist Rachael Whiteread's works, including *Ghost* and *House*, which look like inside-out buildings. In this project, children are able to see the walls and windows of their model revealed the opposite way around when the mould is removed.

Model-making

Approach

1. To create a mould for a block of flats, give each child a piece of card 40 cm long × 25 cm wide. Ask them to measure the halfway point and draw a line with a ruler. Get them to measure the quarter points and draw those lines in. Using their ruler as a guide have them bend the card and fold along the three drawn lines to make four panels.

Resources
- Card
- Rulers
- Art straws
- PVA glue
- Petroleum jelly
- Duct tape or gaffer tape
- Plastic tray
- 2 L plastic pouring jug
- Water
- Plastic cups
- Plaster of Paris
- Spoons for stirring
- Poster paint

Community Buildings

2. Using smaller pieces of card and paper art straws, build up the details of each building, gluing on the pieces with PVA glue.

3. Once dry, smear on a thin coat of petroleum jelly. This will keep the card and plaster separate. Tape the edges of the card together as securely as possible to prevent liquid escaping. (Children may need help with this.)

4. Make a base by drawing around the bottom of the building on a piece of card. Cut out the base and tape securely to the building mould.

5. To make a mould with a pointed rooftop, repeat Steps 1–3. Fold a length of card in half and tape on as a 'V' to the square. Add extra card to make a complete mould.

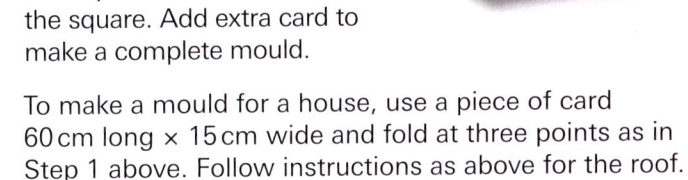

6. To make a mould for a house, use a piece of card 60 cm long × 15 cm wide and fold at three points as in Step 1 above. Follow instructions as above for the roof.

7. For the plaster casting, place the mould in a plastic tray to catch any spillage.

8. To make the plaster, fill the 2 L jug three-quarters full with water. Use a plastic cup to sprinkle the plaster of Paris into the water, without stirring. Continue until a peak of powder begins to appear at the surface of the water. Once a peak appears, slowly stir with a spoon in a circular motion. The liquid should resemble single cream with no lumps. Children can work in pairs but must be supervised.

9. Without delay, pour the liquid plaster into the opening of the mould. Once it is full, tap lightly all around the mould to release any trapped air. Small bubbles will rise to the top. The piece will cure (set) within minutes, but leave to set firmly for at least a week before peeling off the cardboard sides carefully.

10. Ask children to paint the exterior of their buildings with poster paints in a colour of their choice. The exteriors pictured were painted with one colour in four shades, adding different amounts of white paint to each side.

Cross-curricular links

Geography: draw a 2D map of your local area and add it on your 3D models.
Literacy: write an account of plaster casting.
Maths: explore capacity and volume of a variety of containers.
Science: research what happens to different materials when you add water.

In the playground

In this project, children need to design a piece of public art for the playground, a place where they can find someone to play with or take time out. For inspiration look at drawings and sculptures by Sir Henry Moore. For the colour stage, look at the work of Michael Craig-Martin and discuss with children how his work might influence the mood of people who see it. The aim of this project is to make an abstract figure that is welcoming and friendly, but which also provides seating and shelter.

Abstract sculptures

Approach

1. Begin by explaining to children that Sir Henry Moore made drawings to show how he wanted his sculptures to appear. Talk about the way his figures become abstract as sculptures and are barely recognisable as figures.

2. Give children a drawing exercise, asking them to show playtime activities such as running, sitting or playing football.

3. To make a friendship stop, place a lump of clay on a board, tray or sheet. Using their hands and modelling tools, ask children to build a figurative but practical model of a 'friendship stop'. It should be a fun place, perhaps with a shelter, seating or a perimeter.

4. Once the clay has fully hardened, use a fine paintbrush to paint the sculptures with bright colours. Brush on a coat of PVA mixture to act as a varnish.

5. To make a display, arrange the sculptures on a 'playground' surface. Children can draw or paint playtime activities in colour and include themselves in the artwork. Or, if possible, photograph the playground from above, stick the prints onto a piece of card and put the models on top.

6. You could also photograph the children in action at playtime, printing the photographs on a small scale, then cutting out and sticking each figure upright on the playground display.

Resources
- Drawing pencils and paper
- Air-drying clay
- Wooden boards, plastic trays or sheets
- Modelling tools
- Paintbrushes
- Bright poster paints
- PVA glue thinned with water
- Colour pencils or crayons
- A1 card

Cross-curricular links

PSHE: talk about healthy relationships and ways to stop bullying in the playground.

Community Buildings

Improving your local play area

Approach

1. Introduce children to the work of Niki de Saint Phalle, who made some fantastic public sculptures in glorious colours and forms. Her sculpture gardens encourage children to play and climb. Use images of her work to inspire children to make relief clay sculptures for a new playground.

2. Show children a presentation of the work of Niki de Saint Phalle and explain that they are going to make small-scale clay sculptures as designs for their own playground.

3. Discuss working with clay. Show children how to roll out a slab of clay and make simple 3D forms that will be used to build up the relief sculpture. Demonstrate how to use slip to glue the clay forms to the base (see page 7, Step 4).

4. To make a circular base, turn the clay board around several times as you roll out the clay. Trim the smooth slab into a circle with a small plate or saucer. Use damp sponges to wipe away any excess clay.

5. Discuss with children how to incise patterns and decorate the relief playground sculptures. Cover the models with plastic bags to keep them moist between sessions.

6. When the models are decorated, leave them to dry out. They will be fragile, so cover with a 'varnish' mixture of half PVA glue, half water to seal them so that they're ready for painting if desired.

7. Make a display with the sculptures.

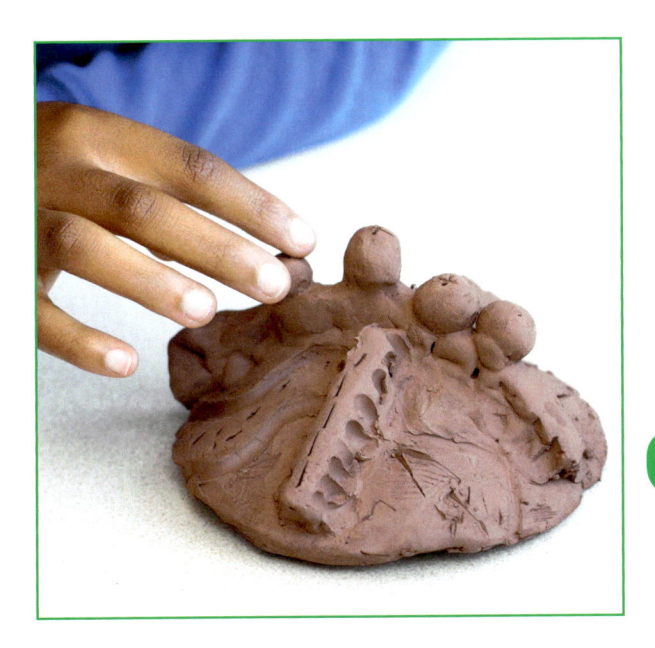

Resources

- Images of work done by Niki de Saint Phalle
- Clay, red earthenware or buff
- Clay boards, wooden slats or boards
- Rolling pins
- Slip (clay and water)
- Modelling tools
- Small plate or saucer
- Damp sponges
- Plastic bags
- PVA glue and water mixture, brushes
- Paints and paintbrushes

Cross-curricular links

History: research children's games a hundred years ago.
Literacy: describe how to improve a nearby playground.

31

A Hindu place of prayer

The Hindu building for communal worship is a mandir and the ornate temples are dedicated to many different gods: Brahma, Vishnu, Shiva, Ganesh, with the head of an elephant, the goddesses Lakshmi, Parvati and many more. At a shrine, many Hindus make an offering of fruit, flowers, incense and water. This brightly-coloured and golden project celebrates the colourful aspects of the religion's imagery.

Collage

Approach

1. Show children images you have researched of temples. Create templates of a curved temple roof and encourage children to draw around these on sheets of paper and cut them out.
2. Ask children to select a small motif from the religious Hindu images the class have looked at. This could be a section of ornate detailing from a shrine or a chrysanthemum and have them draw it on the polyboards, making deep grooves with a blunt pencil. Cut around the motifs, leaving a border around the drawings.
3. Prepare for a printing activity and have children print their motifs all the way around the temple shape. Allow to dry.
4. Encourage children to choose an A4 image of a god or goddess and trace or copy it onto the paper. Paint it using very bright colours. Once dry, cut out and stick in the centre of the temple shape.
5. Surround the god or goddess with gold shapes and make chrysanthemums with orange or yellow tissue paper as an offering. Display on a brightly-coloured background.

Resources
- Images of temples
- Templates of a curved roof
- Drawing pencils
- Large sheets of white paper
- Scissors
- Religious Hindu images, A4 size
- Polyboards, 10 cm × 10 cm
- Blunt pencils
- Black printing ink
- Printing rollers, ink and trays
- Fluorescent or bright paints
- Paints and brushes
- Glue sticks
- Orange or yellow tissue paper

Cross-curricular links

Maths: investigate symmetrical shapes and patterns. Use transformations to create tessellating patterns.

RE: research the Hindu religion and rituals including the symbolism surrounding the Hindu gods.

Community Buildings

A Christian place of worship

Start this project with a visit to a local church to look at architectural details such as arches, the ceiling, the roof, windows and religious imagery. Using a sketchbook or clipboard and paper, ask children to draw what they see. If visiting a church is not possible, children can research famous churches on the internet. St. Paul's and Canterbury cathedrals are traditional and grand, while Liverpool cathedral is more modern. All have very different styles. Children can take elements from each.

Stained-glass

Approach

1. Ask children to look at their church sketches, or at images of church interiors in books or on the internet and get them to select a detailed area of interest.

2. Fold the A2 paper twice to the size of a sheet of A4 paper and open it up again.

3. Using a black crayon, enlarge one of the sketches or part of it and draw it in one A4 section of the sheet.

4. Continue this on each of the four sections of the sheet, referring to a different drawing each time.

5. Select various colours of tissue paper and cut and stick onto the drawings. If the paper goes over the drawing, trace the outline underneath. Brush over the tissue paper with a thin layer of PVA glue to create shine and a stained-glass effect.

6. Repeat the process for each drawing. It is not necessary to fill in the whole drawing, as there will be a nice contrast between drawn and collaged areas.

Resources
- Sketchbooks or clipboards and A4 paper
- Drawing pencils
- A2 cartridge paper
- Black crayons
- Tissue paper in various colours
- Glue sticks
- PVA glue, thinned with water
- Brushes

Cross-curricular links

Literacy: write the story of a young pilgrim who is travelling to Canterbury cathedral.

RE: explore the special features of churches. Research the symbolism and ritual of Christianity.

The mosque and Islamic architecture

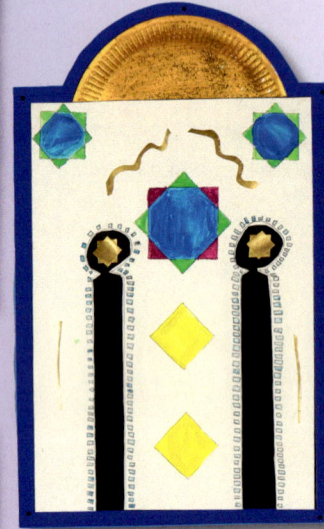

Beautiful mosques and palaces of Southern Spain such as the Alhambra or the Blue Mosque in Istanbul, Turkey are a great starting point to explore the wonders of Islamic architecture. These architects gave great thought and energy to the harmonising effects of symmetry and the calmness that curves and arches provide. Islam does not include the worship of images of the human form, so pattern, calligraphy and mosaic have evolved to a fine art. This project involves a focus on detail, balance and refinement.

Pattern-making

Approach

1. Look at a wide selection of Islamic patterns. To prepare for pattern-making, cut out a selection of square templates of different sizes from stiff paper.

2. Start at the bottom of the A3 paper, drawing two columns with a bulbous dome at the top of each. Next, draw small squares around the edges of the columns. Paint them blue like the typical mosaic tiles seen in Islamic architecture.

3. Using a template, draw a square. Use the same template to draw a diamond shape on top of the square.

4. Create patterns based on Islamic designs. Paint the patterns using colours typical of mosques, earthen colours such as sienna and ochre, green, gold and blue.

5. Cut out the column shapes and glue the painting onto a sheet of black sugar paper, taking care to line up both sheets together.

6. For the mosque dome, cut a paper plate in half and paint it gold. Sprinkle on gold glitter for added shimmer and stick the plate under the top edge of the picture with PVA glue. Stick the mosque on a sheet of dark blue paper with a border all the way around and display on a sheet of pale blue backing paper.

Resources
- Selection of Islamic patterns
- Scissors
- Stiff paper
- A3 cartridge paper
- Drawing pencils
- Water-colour paints and brushes
- Glue sticks
- A3 black sugar paper
- Paper plates
- Gold metallic paint
- Gold glitter
- PVA glue
- Blue backing paper
- Dark blue paper

Cross-curricular links
RE: research the religion of Islam.

Community Buildings

A Buddhist temple

This project takes inspiration from the monumental temples in China, using a bold palette of red, which means good fortune and luck. It also uses gold, an imperial colour which means wealth and happiness in Chinese culture. These temples, like many religious buildings, appear as places of calm and contemplation. The use of symmetry contributes to this, as does the wide and low temple entrance and the presence of the golden Buddha.

Resources
- Strips or blocks of coloured paper: red, yellow, orange, brown, gold
- Glue sticks
- A3 black paper
- Drawing pencils
- A4 gold paper
- Scissors
- Glue sticks
- A4 coloured paper
- PVA glue

3D paper symmetry

Approach

1. For all parts of the temple, children can combine their own choice of colours from the resources list. To make the temple front, create a long rectangle from strips of coloured paper. Some children may want to use blocks instead of strips. Stick onto the sheet of A3 black paper. Add vertical columns and decorative arches.

2. Draw and cut out a Buddha from gold paper and stick in the centre of the temple entrance.

3. To make the roof, cut out two large right-angled triangles from A4 coloured paper, one right and one left facing. A quick way is to cut an A4 sheet of paper diagonally. Fold upwards, concertina style and trim as necessary. Apply PVA glue to the back of the bottom strip of the paper and dab more glue on the folds. Put in place right and left, to form the rooftop. Do not flatten.

4. You could add another row of columns or a strip of colour and repeat the process, this time making the rooftops narrower.

Cross-curricular links

Geography: create a project on China, drawing maps to show the climate, mountains and rivers.
Literacy: write an account of growing up in China today.
RE: research the beginning of Buddhism.

The Ancient World

Aztec totem statues

Statues and stone sculptures by the Aztecs were used as part of worship in and around their temples and city walls. Terrific stone sculptures of gods, warriors and other symbols are the inspiration for these totem-style models. They are in cube form, so children can stack and shift them around. Ancient Aztec culture has many symbols and images that children can use as ideas for decorating their totem carvings.

Clay totems

Approach

1. Ask children to place a lump of clay onto the plastic sheet or tray and form a rough cube with their hands. For flat and even edges, tap each side of the cube a few times in rotation on the tray. This process will help to achieve some uniformity and the models will stack and balance better if the sides are level.

2. Ask children to choose an Aztec symbol for inspiration and use small amounts of clay rolled into fine sausage shapes and balls to press onto a side of the cube. (Cross-hatching and a little water will help to make the clay stick). Use the modelling tools to make designs in the clay.

3. Repeat for three more sides, with a new symbol each time. Gently tap each decorated side, flattening the added pieces well to stop them falling off once dry.

4. Leave the tops and bottoms of each block free of added clay, so that they can be stacked. Decorate simply with the clay tools. It is a good idea for children to scratch their initials into the base.

5. Each child should make a maximum of four blocks.

6. Paint each block white. Then decorate in colour, using a very fine brush, adding any metallic highlights last. If any bits do fall off, simply paint the design back onto the block.

Resources
- Air-drying clay
- Water (if needed)
- Plastic tray or sheet
- Modelling tools
- Poster paint in colours such as white, turquoise, black, dark orange, ochre, gold
- Paintbrushes

Cross-curricular links

Geography: research where and how the Aztecs lived.
History: research why the Aztec Empire collapsed.

The Ancient World

Ancient Greek columns

The architecture of ancient Greece has influenced building design across the world. In Britain, there are 'classical' columns in front of the British Museum, the National Gallery and many town halls, theatres and universities across the country. The Greeks originated three main styles of columns: Ionic, Doric and Corinthian. This project is based on the coiled design of an Ionic column. It's easy and fun to do and can be adapted using string for the roof instead of paper.

String creations

Approach

1. Divide the black paper into four sections for the columns. Children can do this by first making a small pinch at the halfway mark on the paper, then making a pinch mark on either side to make four equal spaces for each column.

2. In the first section use glue to 'draw' the top part of the column and coil lengths of string to make the scroll-like pattern. Space four lengths of string equally to form the rest of the column structure and glue in place. Repeat to make four columns.

3. To make the temple roof, draw and cut out a low-rise triangle from white paper and glue above the four columns, leaving a small gap.

4. Use a black writing pen to draw the straight-edged spiral pattern that is typical in Grecian art.

5. To complete, draw one or more favourite Greek gods or goddesses within the temple roof.

Resources
- A2 black sugar paper
- PVA glue
- Thick string
- Drawing pencils
- A2 white paper
- Black writing pens

Cross-curricular links

History: research the ancient Greek civilisation and find out more about ancient buildings such as the Parthenon.
Literacy: research, retell and update one of the Greek myths.
Maths: the Greeks were great mathematicians. Research terms with a Greek origin, for example, polygon.

37

At home in Benin

In this project, children can describe daily life in ancient Benin with a model village. Starting with a house and its dwellers, the project can be extended to include the double-walled city of Benin. Benin was a wealthy and powerful state in West Africa with a ruling Oba (king), his palace, a marketplace and the inhabitants.

Model-making

Approach

1. To make the houses, bend a piece of cardboard in half to make a pointed roof. Make two more bends to make the short sides of the building. Cut a doorway on one side.

2. Stick strips of masking tape to connect both sides and hold the house in shape. Line up lolly sticks on a sheet of paper (the number depends on the size of the house). Put PVA glue along both bottom edges of the house and stick on top of the lolly sticks. The paper will prevent the floor of the house from sticking to the table.

3. Spread PVA glue on one side of the roof and stick on lolly sticks from one side to the other. Repeat for the other side of the roof.

4. Spread the sides of the house with PVA glue and press on lengths of cut string.

5. Make the people and their clothes out of pipe cleaners. Make a cooking pot by coiling a pipe cleaner and stuffing in a little tissue paper. Glue in place.

6. To make palm trees, roll a piece of orange or brown paper or card and sticky tape together. Cut three to five palm leaves from green tissue paper, dab a little PVA glue on the ends and put into the tree trunk. Once dried, stick them next to the edge of the house.

7. Children can develop the project by creating a city. For example, make a large cardboard base and draw roads on it. Use paper in different colours for the roads, perimeter walls, the palace at the centre and vegetation.

Cross-curricular links

Geography: research the area in and around Benin.
Literacy: write a first-person account of a visit to the ancient city of Benin.

Resources

- Cardboard
- Scissors
- Masking tape
- Lolly sticks
- PVA glue
- Thick string
- Pipe cleaners
- Green tissue paper
- Orange or brown and other colours of paper or card
- Sticky tape

The Ancient World

Benin palace bronzes

Ancient Benin, which is now geographically part of Nigeria, was a walled city. Although most of the ancient city is lost, some remains of the city walls can be seen in the form of mounds in between the new homes there today. Artworks that remain from this period include the Benin Bronzes that adorned the columns within the palace grounds. The images detailed in the Benin Bronzes are largely of powerful soldiers in their finest warrior attire designed to humble any visitor to the palace. The following project involves children making their own Benin Bronzes, using recycled plastic.

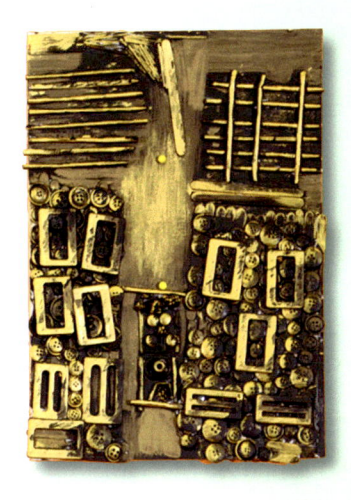

Painting bronzes

Approach

1. Assemble lolly sticks, headless matchsticks, buttons, plastic items and cardboard scraps. Have children look closely at an image of one of the Benin Bronzes. Get them to begin to glue plastic pieces onto card panels, to make their own versions. Use generous amounts of PVA glue so that the pieces stay attached.

2. Once dry, mix together black and brown paint until it is a very dark brown colour. Paint over the panel, covering every detail.

3. Once dry, use bronze paint to highlight features and details to make them stand out. Allow to dry. Allow children to brush gold paint on parts that they wish to emphasise, but use sparingly.

Resources
- Lolly sticks
- Headless matchsticks
- Buttons and plastic items
- Cardboard scraps
- Image of a Benin Bronze
- Stiff card or cardboard panel, A4 or A3 size
- PVA glue
- Black and brown acrylic paint or poster paint mixed with PVA
- Paintbrushes
- Bronze and gold paint

Cross-curricular links

Art: compare royal portraiture to that of the Tudor portraits and the Benin Bronzes.
Geography: research the climate, features and major industries of Nigeria.
History: research the arrival of the first Europeans to Benin.
Literacy: describe the life of a warrior from ancient Benin.

Pyramid-inspired printmaking

This project explores varied and dynamic patterns based on the majestic pyramids that lie in the Egyptian desert. Investigate the natural and earthy colours of ochre, sienna, turquoise, olive green yellow and black, as found in ancient Egyptian paintings. From this starting point, children can create a huge variety of triangular patterns and inventive colour combinations.

Print creations

Approach

1. Have children use a piece of polyboard as the base for their first printing block. Cut a scrap of polyboard into small pieces and arrange these on the first board in a pattern. Repeat this pattern at least twice and glue in place.

2. On the second, same-sized board, draw the pattern from the first board, adding extra detail. Side by side, the boards should be similar.

3. For printing, use paler colours such as light blue, ochre and yellow first and print on the cartridge paper, filling the sheet with four prints from top to bottom in one colour only. Print techniques can be found on page 42.

4. Once dry, take the other print block with the pieces stuck on it and use darker colours such as sienna, black, dark blue and dark orange. Use each colour to print in turn so each print is overlaid on top of the first series of prints.

Cross-curricular links

Geography: research the River Nile looking at its location, where it flows, its uses and problems.

History: look at everyday life in ancient Egypt as shown in tomb paintings.

Science: explore the history of paint. What can you use to make a mark?

Resources
- Two 15 cm × 6 cm polyboards
- Polyboard off-cuts and scraps
- Scissors
- Glue sticks
- Drawing pencils
- Printing inks and blocks
- Rollers and trays
- A3 cartridge paper

The Ancient World

Columns for a pharaoh's palace

The monumental palaces and temples of ancient Egypt were built on a vast scale and were adorned with beautiful and elaborate frescos. The columns that stand boldly in front of these structures show the pharaohs and gods and are carved and painted with great skill. Children can explore this art and create their own Egyptian motifs to carve a column fit for a pharaoh.

Resources
- One polyboard panel, 30 cm × 10 cm
- One polyboard panel, 15 cm × 15 cm
- Blunt pencils
- Rulers
- Scissors
- Black acrylic paint
- Sponges
- PVA glue and brushes
- Dry sand

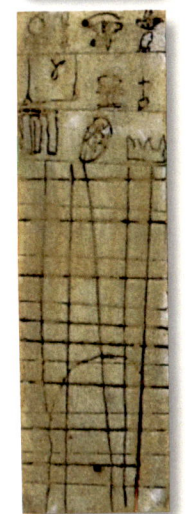

Motifs and carvings

Approach

1. On the larger polyboard panel, ask children to draw a pattern based on designs found in ancient Egyptian art, such as figures in profile or hieroglyphs. They can use a ruler to create geometric designs.

2. On the smaller polyboard panel, draw a fat T-shape tapering to 10 cm in width and cut it out. This is the capital or top section of the column. Draw a detailed design on it. Darken the grooves drawn into the polyboard by smearing in a little black acrylic paint with a sponge. Wash the sponge and immediately wipe away as much of the excess paint as possible before it dries.

3. Spread PVA glue all over both pieces of board and press face down into a tray of dry sand. Repeat as necessary until the whole surface is covered and tap on the side of the tray to remove any excess sand.

4. Display with the T-shape capital on top of the column.

Cross-curricular links

History: research the Egyptian animal gods.
Literacy: iInvent your own alphabet using pictograms and write a message for the class to decode.
Maths: research the Egyptian number system and the symbols they used. What number did they not have a symbol for?

41

Pyramids brick by brick

Maths and surface pattern design are combined in this project to produce a textured pyramid that is fit for the Egyptian desert. Each side of the square-based pyramid should show a different texture, material and creative process by exploring tessellation and brick patterns in four different ways. Start by asking children to look at brickwork in the local area. What about the school playground walls? Sketch the way bricks are put together and photograph the brickwork, to use as part of the project.

Nets and patterns

Approach

1. On a large sheet of flexible card, encourage children to draw a net (plan) of a pyramid and cut it out. The ones pictured have a square base 30 cm × 30 cm with flaps at the edges so they can be assembled. Children can use this as a template for further pyramids.
2. On each triangle facia, demonstrate the following techniques.
3. On a piece of polyboard, draw a brick pattern with a pencil, creating deep grooves.
4. Squeeze a length of ochre printing ink into the top end of the tray. Dip the roller lightly into the ink and roll the roller up and down until a 'sticky' sound is heard, leaving most of the ink intact at the top. Once the roller is evenly covered, roll over the print block until it too is evenly covered.

The Ancient World

5. Press the board evenly onto the bottom corner of the triangle. Lift to reveal the image and repeat the process until the triangle is covered with prints.

6. To make a photo montage, take pictures of a brick wall and print the pictures in colour. Cut the photos into pieces and stick them onto a new triangle with a glue stick. Avoid leaving gaps between the cut pieces and overlap to combine different textures.

7. To create a collage, cut gold paper into small rectangles and stick onto a triangle.

8. To make sandy bricks, cut cardboard (box card) into small rectangles and brush each one with PVA glue. Place glue-side down into a tray of sand and put aside to dry. Use generous amounts of PVA to glue each sandy brick onto the final triangle.

9. If your pyramid is large, assemble with a glue gun (adult only). This will hold each side together instantly. For smaller pyramids, children can dab PVA glue along the flaps and hold it together temporarily with masking tape while it bonds.

Resources
- Flexible card in any colour
- Drawing pencils
- Scissors
- Polyboard, 10 cm × 6 cm
- Ochre printing ink, tray, roller and print block
- Photographs of brickwork
- Glue sticks
- Gold paper
- Cardboard (box card)
- Brush and PVA glue or glue gun (adult use only)
- Tray of sand
- Masking tape

Cross-curricular links

History: research how the pyramids were built.

Maths: explore nets to make different solid shapes.

Science: find out how materials change under pressure.

43

Chinese houseboats

This project involves creating a serene picture of a boat at sea using techniques from Chinese art. The houseboat is based on the Chinese junk, which was developed during the Han Dynasty as far back as 206 BC. These boats were used to explore the oceans from China to India as well as Africa. For inspirational sunsets, show children work by artists William Turner and Claude Monet, who used violets to hot reds and bright yellows. Also look at Chinese art painted with brush and ink in their colour palettes, of images such as cherry blossom trees and fish.

Chinese art techniques

Approach

1 Using a large paintbrush, spread water across the cartridge paper and then lightly brush sunset colours, for example, of pink, yellow and red onto the damp surface, taking time to let the colours spread naturally across the paper.

2 On black paper, draw and cut out a silhouette of a junk boat hull and sails separately. Once the sunset background is dry, glue the junk boat on or below the horizon line.

3 Thin some black paint with a little water. Use a fine brush to add birds, blossom trees and fish.

Resources
- Brushes
- A3 cartridge paper
- Watercolour paints, black, red, orange, yellow, pink, fluorescents if possible
- Black paper
- Drawing pencil
- Scissors
- Glue sticks
- Black paint and water

Cross-curricular links

Geography: draw a map of Marco Polo's travels.
History: research the journey of Marco Polo to China.
Literacy: give a first-person account of a trip in a junk across the sea to Africa.
Maths: use a map scale to measure the distance by sea from China to Africa.

The Ancient World

The Great Wall of China

The Great Wall of China is the longest man-made structure in the world. It crosses some of the most rugged and mountainous parts of China and was built to keep out invaders from the Mongol region, for example, Genghis Khan. The Great Wall was constructed over a very long period of time: from the 5th century BC until the 16th century AD, when the last pieces were added. If possible, show the class images of the wall taken from space by NASA. In this project, each child is to make a section of the wall and all the sections are to be assembled to form an entire wall.

Resources
- Dry penne pasta
- Poster paints
- Brushes
- Metallic paint (optional)
- A3 cartridge paper
- PVA glue

Frieze

Approach

1. Ask children to paint a generous quantity of dry pasta light brown. Paint some pasta in metallic colours and put to one side.
2. On A3 paper (portrait), have each child draw a mountain or hillside halfway or one-third of the way down the sheet.
3. Ask each child to paint a blue sky, white clouds, and use greens and browns for the mountains.
4. Using the painted pasta and generous amounts of PVA glue, build a wall along the top of the mountain with a combination of coloured pasta pieces. Remember it should look like a strong fort that will keep invaders out.
5. Assemble all the sheets of paper in a long frieze.

Cross-curricular links

Geography: look at the extent of the Great Wall on a map.
History: research Chinese architecture over the past 500 years. How has the architectural style changed?
Literacy: imagine you are part of Genghis Khan's invading force. Describe an attack on the Great Wall of China.
Maths: work out how much time it would take to walk or run the extent of the Great Wall of China.

Architecture in Stories

A chocolate factory for Charlie

Roald Dahl leaves Charlie's fantastic chocolate factory to the imagination of his readers, wisely knowing that they will have many ideas of their own. In this project, children can use 3D shapes as building blocks to build any kind of city – real or futuristic.

3D design and construction techniques

Approach

1. Read Roald Dahl's *Charlie and the Chocolate Factory* with children, discussing the factory with them. Show them a presentation about mass production. *How do children think the wonderful sweets were made? What sweets do they like?* Ask them to draw sweets designs on paper with marker pens and write lists of what they would include in their own chocolate factory. Add to coloured card to make a display.

2. Get children to make cylinders, cubes, cuboids and spheres out of A4 paper and use them to build all sorts of constructions.

3. Demonstrate cutting an A4 sheet of paper into three pieces (see diagram at right). Use each of the three pieces to make a different-sized cylinder of different heights and widths. Using a pencil placed on the end of one piece, roll the paper into a cylinder and glue along the edge to secure. Discuss how to make the cylinders stand up and demonstrate cutting into the base of each cylinder to create flaps. Glue the cylinders onto an A4 card base.

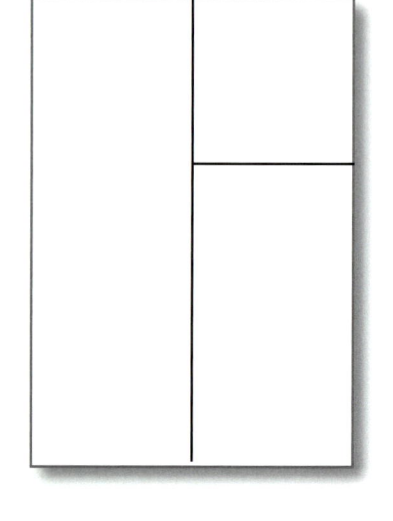

Architecture in Stories

Resources
- *Charlie and the Chocolate Factory* by Roald Dahl
- Presentation about factories
- A4 paper
- Marker pens
- Scissors
- Pencils
- Glue sticks or PVA glue
- A4 card bases
- Masking tape
- A4 paper cutter and single-hole punch (adult use only)
- Paper fasteners
- Colour card
- Collage materials: pipe cleaners, buttons, sweet wrappers, glitter, glue pens

4. Use one sheet of A4 paper to make a tall cuboid. Fold the paper in half vertically and in half again so that there are four equal rectangular pieces. Unfold and stand up to make an open cuboid. To join the cuboid, use masking tape or a narrow strip of paper 2–3 cm wide, folded in half to form a hinge that can be glued. Discuss how to make the cuboid stand up. A triangular prism must be folded into three equal pieces.

5. Ask children to make spheres. An adult should use a paper cutter to slice A4 paper into strips. In the middle of each strip, punch a hole with a single-hole punch. Get children to continue to place a paper fastener through the hole. Add more strips and join them at the top until they have enough strips to fan them out into a circle. Attach at the bottom to make a sphere.

6. Encourage children to create factory structures using coloured card, working in groups.

7. Decorate the factory structures with collage items and add to the display.

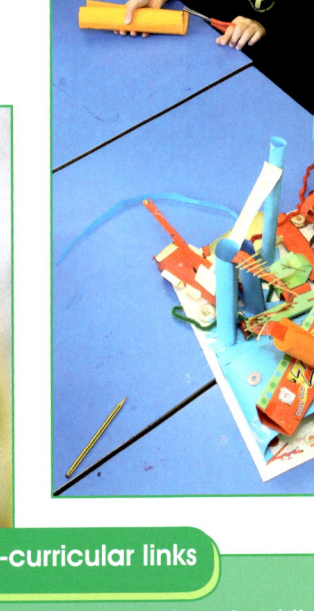

Cross-curricular links
Drama: write a play about the reopening of Willy Wonka's factory.
Geography: research where chocolate comes from. Where is it grown and how is it harvested?
Literacy: invent a new and amazing food.
Maths: solve problems to work out how many sweets a factory can make in an hour/day/week/month year if they make a certain number every second.
Science: what foods are good for us?

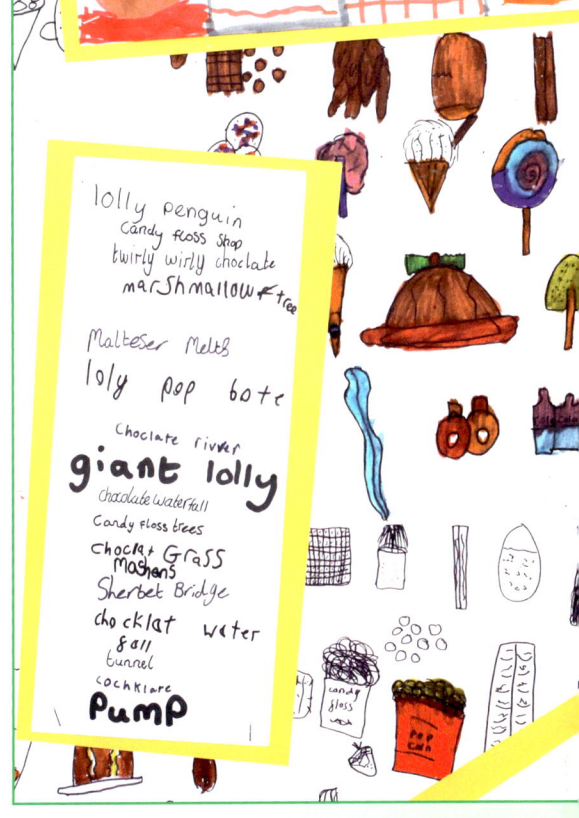

Hansel and Gretel gingerbread house

This project recreates the famous gingerbread house from one of the best-known fairytales by the Grimm brothers. Children will make their own house, fill it with irresistible-looking 'sweets', and varnish it for a sugar-glaze effect. They can use the finished piece to tell this grim Grimm fairytale. Encourage them to tempt their friends' tummies with their special fairytale creations!

Resources
- Cardboard, about 40 cm × 25 cm
- Drawing pencils
- Scissors
- Strips of white card
- Paper art straws (optional)
- Mixing bowls
- Salt dough: 2 cups of plain flour, 1 cup each of salt and water
- Poster paints in bright colours
- Paintbrushes
- PVA glue and water

⚠ **Make sure children do not eat the 'sweets'.**

Fairytale creations

Approach

1. To make the house, draw the shape of a house onto cardboard with a pointed roof. Cut it out. Use card strips to make a door and two windows.
2. To make the sweets and treats from salt dough, mix together the flour, salt and water in a bowl. The consistency should be dough-like and pliable. If it sticks to the fingers, sprinkle in a little more flour. The recipe should make enough dough for 'sweets' for four children.
3. Break off small pieces and model into different shapes of 'sweets'. Once they are completely dry and hard, paint each piece with candy colours.
4. Use generous amounts of PVA glue to stick the sweets on the house. Allow them to dry.
5. To give the house a sugar-glaze effect, add a little water to some PVA glue and brush over the entire piece.

Cross-curricular links

History: research the origin of one of the other Grimm fairytales.
Literacy: write a play based on *Hansel and Gretel* and act it out in class.
PSHE: discuss stranger danger with children and talk about which adults they can trust.
Science: examine why fizzy, sugary drinks are bad for teeth.

Architecture in Stories

Indian tales

This project is about shapes and patterns, and how to recognise patterns in architecture. Show children images of Indian houses and books of Indian folk stories, for example, *Stories from India* by Anna Milbourne, or *Elephant Dance: A Journey to India* by Theresa Heine, or *The Tiger Child* by Joanna Troughton. Talk about the rich variety of buildings.

Resources
- A3 and A1 paper
- Marker pens
- Stories and images of Indian homes
- Oil pastels
- A4 card
- Glue sticks
- Stapler (adult use only)
- Battery-operated fairy lights (optional)

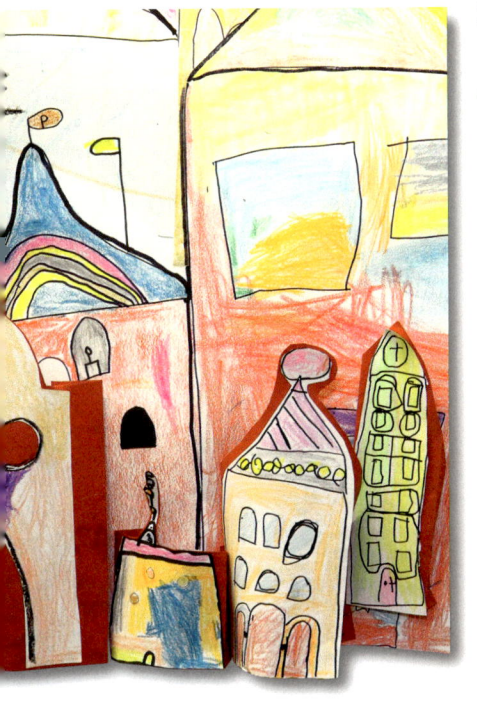

Building patterns

Approach

1. Explain to children that a pattern has something in it that is repeated. Ask children to look for patterns in the classroom. *Can they see colour patterns? Can they see shape patterns?*

2. Hand out sheets of A3 paper and demonstrate how to fold the paper in three, to make four equal strips. Use marker pens and ask children to draw examples of patterns around them. Encourage them to create their own patterns.

3. Tell children that adding colour to the patterns will create new patterns. Use children's pattern strips as a border for the final display.

4. Read children stories from India and show them photographs of the different kinds of Indian homes. Discuss the houses and talk about the shapes and colours of the buildings. What patterns can they see? Working in groups, with marker pens and A1 paper, children should draw their own Indian buildings. Let them add their own colours with oil pastels. These large drawings will make the backdrop for the display.

5. To complete the display, have children make stand-up cards. Using A4 card with a centre panel, glue cut-out drawings of small-scale buildings on the centre panel. An adult should staple the cards to the display with the middle panel sticking out to create a 3D effect. Add a string of battery-operated fairy lights to switch on at story time.

Cross-curricular links

Geography: research a project about India and Indian culture.
Maths: create tessellating patterns using a variety of 2D shapes.

49

The old woman who lived in a shoe

The story of "The old woman who lived in a shoe" is a stimulus for a lot of creative opportunities for young children.

Resources
- "The old woman who lived in a shoe" nursery rhyme
- Adult shoes or boots
- Marker pens
- A3 size, good quality paper
- Scissors
- Sticky tape or masking tape
- Lengths of sticky-backed brown paper tape
- Glue stick or PVA glue
- Collage materials such as sequins and googly eyes
- Pipe cleaners
- Single-hole punch (adult use only)

Designing a fairytale home

Approach

1. Start by reading "The old woman who lived in a shoe". Talk about how children could use a shoe as a house.

2. Hand out A3 paper and talk about the outline shape of the shoe or boot before providing black marker pens for drawing. Talk about who lives in the shoe.

3. Explain to children that they should take off one shoe, put it in the middle of an A3 sheet of paper and draw around the outline. An adult should score the shoe outline with scissors.

4. Make cuts at intervals from the edge of the paper up to the shoe outline and all the way around. Fold the flaps of paper, beginning at the front of the shoe. Stick them together with tape so that they look like slippers. Fold the flaps at the heel end of the shoe and tape onto the sole. At this point, children should try on their shoe to make sure it fits.

5. Strengthen the shoe by covering it with a layer of cut pieces of sticky-backed brown paper tape.

6. Children can decorate them with collage materials. Pipe cleaners can be threaded through holes made with a single-hole punch to create laces.

Cross-curricular links

Literacy: write a story about the creatures who live in the shoes that have been made.

Maths: make a bar chart of shoe sizes in the class.

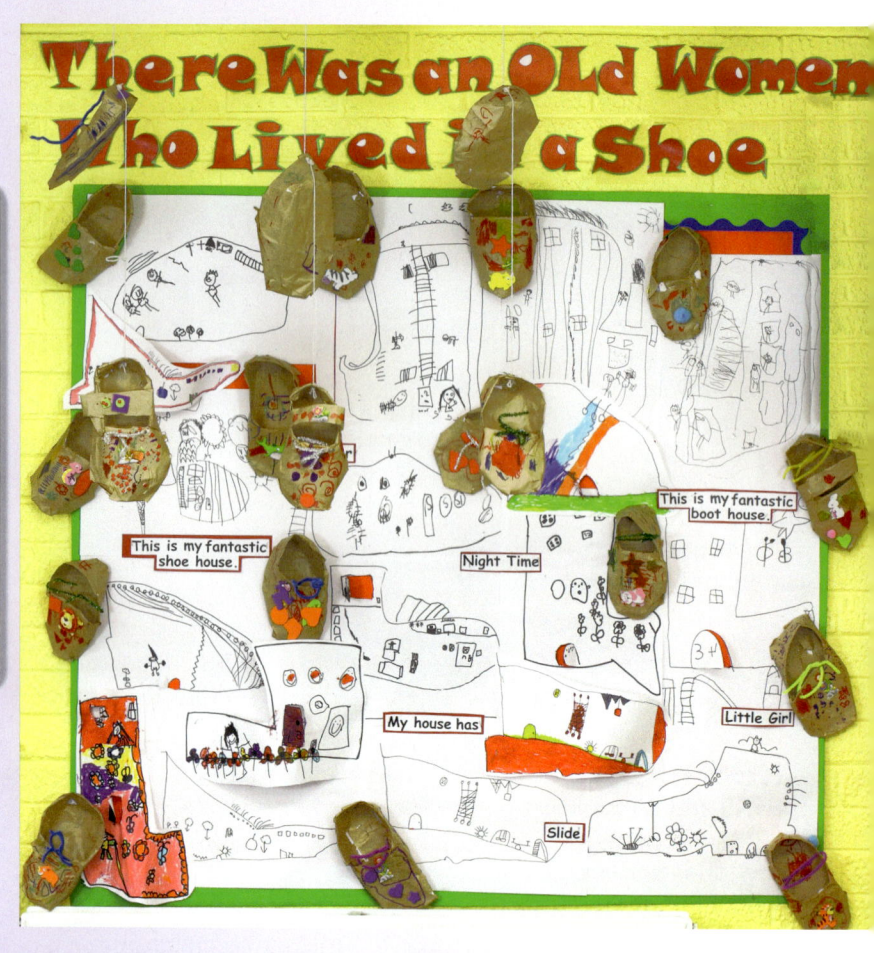

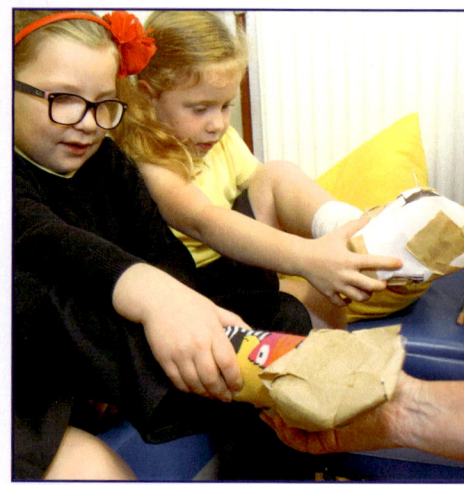

Architecture in Stories

Tightrope between the towers

This project is about recreating the magical part of the true story of Philippe Petit. Petit spent an hour dancing and performing tricks on a tightrope a quarter of a mile in the sky between the twin towers of the World Trade Center in New York.

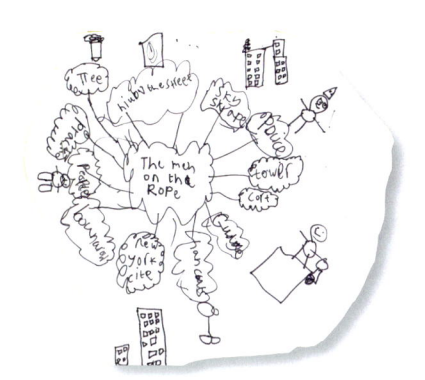

Mind maps and model-making

Approach

1. Read from and talk about *The Man Who Walked Between the Towers*, showing Mordicai Gerstein's illustrations. Talk about any ideas children have for making models. A good way to recall a story with young children is to ask them to draw mind maps with pictures. They can include these in the final display together with drawings and models.

2. Ask children to make their own drawings of skyscrapers.

3. Get children to choose a box, and to work in pairs, so each makes their own tower on a shared coloured card base. Begin by securing any flaps on the boxes with masking tape. Stand the box upright and demonstrate wrapping coloured card around the box, carefully pressing and pinching along the edges. Glue in place before trimming the top. Stick on the windows cut out of shiny paper.

4. Show children how to glue small pieces of photocopied mind maps to their base to help them draw their new maps. When finished, have children decide where to put their buildings, gluing them down with small hinges of card. They should measure the distance between their towers and cut a length of string to stretch across. Tape the string and glue a matching piece of coloured card to camouflage the tape.

Resources
- *The Man Who Walked Between the Towers* by Mordicai Gerstein
- A3 and A4 paper
- Marker pens
- Small boxes
- Masking tape
- A4 coloured card
- Glue sticks
- Scissors
- Shiny paper
- Rulers or measuring tapes
- String

Cross-curricular links

Geography: find out about other buildings in New York.
Literacy: describe how you might feel, walking on a tightrope, 100 metres in the air.
PE: practise some balancing activities in the school grounds.

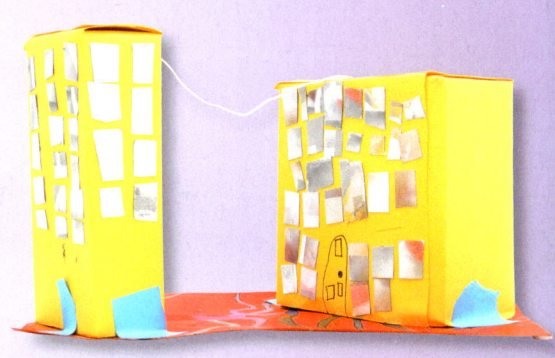

51

At home with The Twits

As in the very funny conclusion of *The Twits* by Roald Dahl, in this project children can show this snapshot into the chaotic home of Mr and Mrs Twit right way up or upside down!

3D characters

Approach

1. Paint the inside of the box lid in a bright colour and put to one side.

2. To make Mr and Mrs Twit, cut out two small pieces of card and glue at the top of two lolly sticks to make faces for Mr and Mrs Twit. Stick on googly eyes or buttons with PVA glue.

3. For arms, twist a pipe cleaner around each lolly stick, dabbing glue on both sides to hold it in place. Use scraps of felt glued in place to dress scruffy Mr and Mrs Twit. Tie a twig into Mr Twit's hand as his walking stick.

4. Put a blob of glue at the top of each head, and snap twigs to short lengths. One by one, carefully place the end of each twig in the glue, building up the hair. Repeat on Mr Twit's chin to create a scruffy beard. Leave flat and undisturbed to dry firm.

5. Create the Twits' scruffy house by cutting out chair and table shapes from black paper, and glue in place. Then put a generous amount of glue on the back of the characters and glue them into position.

6. Wipe glue on one end of a twig and balance on the edge of the lid. Children may need help with balancing the twigs. Then leave the twigs to dry undisturbed.

Resources

- Shoebox lids or similar
- Poster or acrylic paints
- Paintbrushes
- Scissors
- White cards
- Glue sticks
- PVA glue
- Lolly sticks × 2
- Googly eyes or small buttons
- Pipe cleaners
- Felt scraps
- Fine twigs
- Black paper

Cross-curricular links

History: research the life of Roald Dahl.
Literacy: read other Roald Dahl stories. Which one do you like best and why?

Architecture in Stories

Narnia and eternal winter

This illustrative project takes inspiration from C.S. Lewis' *The Lion, the Witch and the Wardrobe* and combines the wardrobe into which the children climb and the winter forest the children discover on the other side. It presents the two worlds as a folding piece of work. Children can add characters from the story to their scenes.

Fantasy folding work

Approach

1. Cut out a rectangular piece of silver paper or card and fold inwards to make two flaps.

2. To make the wardrobe doors, paint the outside of the two flaps with mid-brown, sienna or ochre paint. Cut out cardboard panels and paint in darker and lighter shades of brown and glue onto the doors.

3. Open the wardrobe doors and start with the White Witch's castle in the centre panel. Glue paper art straws into a spiky arch in the angular-looking castle that could be the home of the evil witch.

4. Spread a layer of PVA glue over the art straws using a brush. Then cover with a piece of foil by starting in the middle and pressing the foil gently from the centre, outwards. Trim off the edges. Paint the foil a frosty blue and wipe away excess paint from the relief with a sponge and tissue (see page 39).

5. To create the forest, arrange the twigs to look like trees and bushes and glue with generous amounts of PVA glue. Add fallen snow to trees and the castle, as well as on the ground with pieces of rolled-up cotton wool.

Resources

- Scissors
- Silver paper or card
- Shades of brown, ochre, sienna and frosty-blue poster paint
- Paintbrushes
- PVA glue
- Paper art straws
- Aluminium foil
- Small sponges and tissues
- Twigs
- Cotton wool

Cross-curricular links

Literacy: write a fantasy story in which you enter another world. How will you get there? Read other stories of parallel worlds.

PSHE: look at moral dilemmas within *The Lion, the Witch and the Wardrobe* and discuss.

Building Britain

Gladiators at the amphitheatre

All over Europe are the hidden remains of amphitheatres that once entertained the public throughout the Roman Empire. The amphitheatre in Rome was the largest. It hosted extravagant shows that included imported animals such as lions, tigers and elephants. However, there was also an amphitheatre in the Roman city of Londinium (now London). While this amphitheatre was much smaller than the one in Rome, its capacity was still large enough to hold a quarter of the city's population at the time. Start this project with exciting action drawings to show children what used to happen in the arena, before moving on to make a model amphitheatre.

Drawing and Modroc models

Approach

1. To make action drawings, take a landscape sheet of A4 coloured paper, and from the top right corner to the top left corner, draw a shallow curve. Turn the sheet around and repeat. Cut out both curves. Draw arches along the lower half of each curve and cut them out. Glue the remaining centre part onto A4 white paper.

2. Draw in the audience, including the Roman nobility. Ask children to use their imagination to draw a fighting scene within the stadium. Encourage them to add speech bubbles to their drawings.

Building Britain

3. To create the amphitheatre wall, fold an A2 sheet of newsprint lengthways so that it is 5–7 cm high. It should almost fit around the circumference of a paper plate. Leave the gap as an entrance. Fix in position with pieces of masking tape.

4. Begin to cover the paper wall inside and out with Modroc strips (see page 22). Cover the inside of the plate and where the wall meets the plate on the outside.

5. Add features such as arches and detailing at the entrance. For the seating, create a series of horseshoe benches. It may take a little time and practice to fold, twist and press the Modroc onto the surface.

6. Once the Modroc is fully hardened, tear the tissue paper and glue on to cover the amphitheatre.

7. To make the gladiators, bend two or three pipe cleaners together to form a simple figure. Reduce each gladiator's height and arm length so that it is stable, and position in a dramatic pose. Dress the gladiators using foil for a helmet, sandals and breast plate. Arm them with button shields. Glue them into position with a glue gun. To add a crowd, have children dip their fingers in paint and make a line of dots along the interior walls of the amphitheatre.

8. If children wobble the amphitheatre it will look as if the gladiators are fighting!

Resources

- A4 coloured paper
- Colour pencils
- Scissors
- Glue sticks
- A4 white paper
- A2 newsprint
- Paper plates
- Masking tape
- Modroc and water
- Tissue paper (earthy colours)
- PVA glue thinned with a little water
- Pipe cleaners
- Aluminium foil
- Large buttons
- Glue gun (adult use only)
- Paint (for crowd)

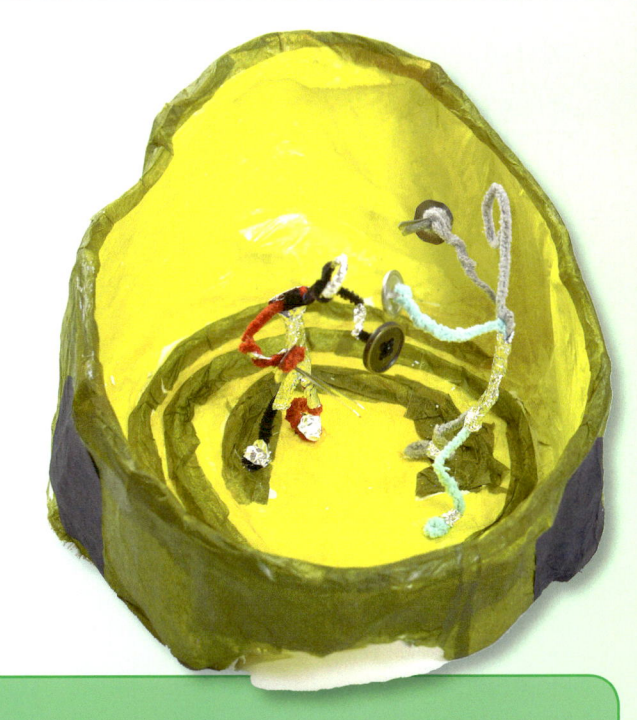

Cross-curricular links

History: research the history of the Romans in Britain and the remains of the buildings they built here.

Literacy: give an eye-witness account of an event in the amphitheatre from the point of view of first a spectator and then a gladiator.

Wattle and daub settlements

This project explores construction methods in Britain before modern technology where children must weave and reinforce walls with their own wattle (wooden strips) and daub (sticky clay or mud) and see for themselves how the process works. Both Celts and early English builders used wattle and daub, and it is still used today in parts of rural India, for example. Children can make smaller versions of the walls pictured here and join the four sides together to make individual buildings.

Weaving and constructing

Approach

1. To create the frame place two sticks parallel to each other. Apply PVA glue to both ends of two lolly sticks and glue one at either end of the sticks to form a thin rectangle. Add more lolly sticks to form a grid, making sure they are evenly spaced.

2. When the glue is dry, use paper art straws to weave in and out of the frame, going under and over the lolly sticks and closing any gaps as you go. Trim any straggly ends.

3. To make the daub, ask children to get into pairs and mix together clay, sand, a squeeze of PVA glue, and some straw or sawdust. Get them to gradually add water, using their fingers to make a mushy mixture. Spread over the frame in a thin layer from left to right, pushing it into any gaps. Put aside to dry.

4. Make a further three frames.

5. To make the roof, cut a line to the centre of a paper plate, bend it into a cone shape and staple into position. If you like, paint the paper plate brown or yellow.

6. Prepare longer pieces of chopped straw. Cover the cone with PVA glue and roll it in the straw.

7. Stand the four frames carefully on a cardboard base (they will be heavy!) and use green modelling material to fix them upright. Glue four roofs together and place on top. The roofs are removable so that you can see inside the hut.

Cross-curricular links

Art: find out more about weaving.

History: research early settlements in Britain.

Resources
- Two thin sticks, about 20 cm in length
- PVA glue
- Lolly sticks
- Paper art straws
- Air-drying clay
- Sand
- Straw, chopped-up, or sawdust
- Water
- Scissors
- Paper plates
- Stapler (adult use only)
- Brown or yellow paint and a paintbrush (optional)
- Cardboard base
- Green modelling material
- Longer pieces of straw

Building Britain

Tower of London hats

The Tower of London stands largely unchanged since it was built by William the Conqueror in 1066. It is famous for the captives held there. Show children close-up images of the tower's architectural features such as turrets, brickwork, round towers, windows, stone carvings, Traitors Gate, arrow slits and ravens, which can add distinct features to its design. Children can start by sketching their ideas before making the hats.

Modelling hats

Approach

1. Dip the side of a scrap piece of card or polyboard into black paint and print horizontal lines across an A1 sheet of flexible card. Use the same process to add shorter vertical lines between the horizontal lines to create a brick pattern.

2. Each sheet will have brickwork of a different size. Cut these sheets into smaller panels as required for the hats, and share for a variety of scales.

3. According to each child's design, they need to bend and fold the panels into a basic shape. Check that each hat fits the wearer.

4. Use PVA glue to secure the panels and hold in position with masking tape or paper clips until the glue dries. Once it's dry, remove the masking tape or paper clips. For any difficult areas use a stapler to secure.

5. Cut out the alternating low and high brickwork at the top of the castle walls. Using black paper, draw, cut out and stick on details of choice such as windows, arches and other features chosen.

6. Add characters such as Henry VIII's queens or the executioner, drawn on white paper and coloured with pencils or watercolours. Add speech bubbles, then cut out and glue to the hat.

7. Children can now model their hats.

Resources
- Scrap card or polyboard
- Black poster or acrylic paint
- A1 flexible white card
- Scissors
- PVA glue
- Masking tape or paper clips
- Stapler (adult use only)
- Black sugar paper
- A4 white paper
- Colour pencils or watercolours and paintbrushes

Cross-curricular links

History: research Tudor kings and queens.
Literacy: keep a diary as a prisoner in the Tower. How would you pass the time?

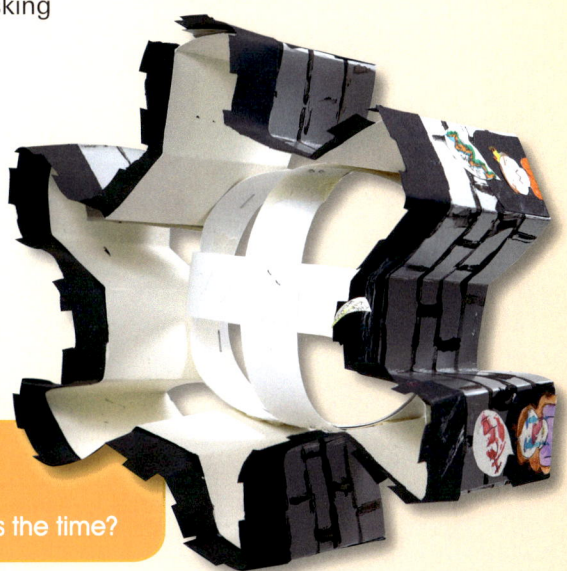

Tudor timber-framed houses

A Tudor building has a distinctive white exterior with black lines on the outside. The black lines are painted wooden beams, which form the structure of the building. Look at these buildings on the internet, visiting them if possible, because some are still standing today. Distorted with age, with sloping doorways and often leaning to one side, they have taken on a charm all of their own. Challenge children by asking them to solve the design problems in this project.

Resources
- Cardboard
- Masking tape
- Craft knife (adult use only)
- Modroc and water
- White paint and brushes
- Black sugar paper
- PVA glue
- Scissors
- Brown or black paper
- Thick string

Modroc constructions

Approach

1. Bend a long rectangular piece of cardboard into four to make a square, and tape to secure. For the pointed roof, take a shorter piece of card of the same width and bend in half. Secure in place above the square.

2. For the interior structure, take a shorter piece of card, bend it in the shape of an arch and slot it snugly within the square frame. Then tape in place. This a good design problem for children, who will enjoy the challenge of making the pieces fit. If they like, children can also make extra rooms with pieces of card by drawing two or three windows on the side of the card. Cut them out with a craft knife.

3. Using Modroc (see page 22), children should smooth the strips with their fingers so that any small holes disappear. Beginning with the lower part of the building, the structure will need two layers. Cover the window frame, smoothing the Modroc just inside to cover the cut edge.

Building Britain

4. Use a layer of large pieces of Modroc to create a plaster wall to cover one of the two open sides. Stretch the Modroc as tightly as possible, although it will sag a little while drying. Turn the model face down on the open side, leaving the plaster side facing upwards. Once dry, paint the whole house white.

5. Stick on strips of black sugar paper with PVA glue to look like a timber frame. Follow a traditional beam pattern, or create a unique design. To add shine, brush each strip with a thin layer of PVA glue that has been thinned with water.

6. For a tiled roof, cut small squares of brown or black paper. Apply glue to the top edge of each square. Press onto the roof, starting at the bottom edge and working upwards.

7. For a thatched roof, spread glue over the roof and have children press on lengths of thick string with their fingers. Repeat on the other side of the roof.

Cross-curricular links

Design and Technology: research load-bearing structures. How do you make things stand up?

Literacy: write an account of life for a child in a Tudor town.

Science: research pulling and pushing forces including gravity.

59

A Victorian school building

This project is a combination of two elements of a Victorian education – a school building and a writing slate on which children of that era learned to read, write and do basic arithmetic. If you are in a Victorian school building, children can sketch the inside of the classroom or hall, or the outside of the building from the playground. They should look at details such as doors and window frames, rooftops and brickwork. Or, search the internet for images of red-brick Victorian schools and discover the way Victorian children lived and learned.

Creating a slate

Approach

1. Using a white oil pastel or crayon, draw the school building, or detail from the building, as large as possible on the black paper, leaving space around the edge.

2. In the spaces above or below the drawing, write simple addition sums or a times table so that it resembles a classroom slate.

3. To create the wood-effect edging of the slate, draw two to three lines along each of the four strips of brown paper to look like wood grain. Add 'knots' by bending the straight lines to accommodate a small circle drawn in-between.

4. Glue on the strips and cut to size, rounding the corners to look like a slate.

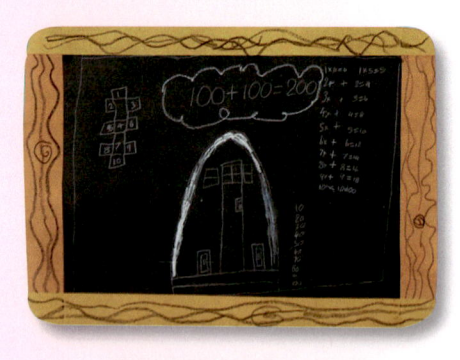

Resources
- White oil pastel or crayon
- A3 black sugar paper
- Brown paper strips
- Black crayon or oil pastels
- Glue sticks
- Scissors

Cross-curricular links

History: how were children treated in the past? How did they learn?

Literacy: research and write about a Victorian school day.

Building Britain

Foggy smoggy top hats

These top hats depict street life in the days of Queen Victoria. Images of rich and poor are good source material, as are the clothes that people wore and images of street sellers, children and toys. Architectural features on a street of townhouses are important, for example, cast-iron street lamps and chimneys belching smoke. Look at pictures of foggy, smoggy dark nights in the city or read a descriptive passage by Charles Dickens.

Making hats

Approach

1. To make a hat, give each child a piece of flexible card and have them put the side of a crayon across the card to make 'fog' marks. Draw a baseline 2 cm from the bottom edge of the card. All the artwork should be attached to the card above this line.

2. On white paper, in pencil or crayon, draw townhouses, carriages and people. Cut out the drawings and glue them onto the 'foggy' background of the hat, leaving some space in between. Layer on drawings of people and carriages and add light to the houses with squares of orange paper glued behind a few window frames.

3. To make street lamps, cut a thin strip from black paper as well as a small rectangle and glue together. Glue on a smaller yellow square and then glue a short horizontal paper strip under the lamp.

4. To assemble the hat, make cuts from the bottom edge of the flexible card to the baseline at 2 cm intervals. Bend back the flaps.

5. An adult should help each child put their hat together and make sure the hat will fit on the child's head. This is done by wrapping the decorated card around the child's head and stapling the card ends together to form the main part of the hat.

6. To make the hat brim, draw a large circle on the flexible card and cut it out. Place the top of the hat in the middle of the circle and draw around it. Cut out the middle circle and use for the top hat. The ring of card remaining will form the brim. Paint the brim black.

7. Fix the brim in place around the middle of the hat. Glue the hat flaps to the brim, preferably with a glue gun. Then fit the top of the hat.

8. Model the hat.

Resources
- Black crayons
- White flexible card
- White cartridge paper
- Pencils
- Scissors
- Fluorescent orange and yellow paper
- PVA glue
- Black sugar paper
- Glue gun (adult use only)
- Black paint and brushes
- Stapler (adult use only)

Cross-curricular links

History: research how street lighting changed life in Victorian times.

Science: investigate electricity and gas power and the invention of the electric light bulb.

Inside a Victorian factory

This project peeks into a grimy factory in Victorian Britain, which was the daily life for thousands of children. Conditions were dirty and hazardous and children were often injured while using heavy machinery. Show children photographs that reflect the grinding poverty and huge industrial buildings where children worked during this era. Also look at L.S. Lowry's paintings of northern towns, which show factory life during the 20th century. If a Victorian building is nearby, photograph the brickwork to use in the project.

3D collage

Approach

1. Bend a piece of card in four places to form a mini-theatre shape.

2. Take photos of an old brick wall and print them in colour. Cut them into pieces and stick them onto the card, lining the inside with the brick prints.

3. Cut rectangles of card and paint them in different shades of brown, similar to those found on brick walls or older buildings. Once dry, stick them onto the outer flaps with PVA glue and allow to dry.

4. For the cogs, paint one or two paper plates black or silver. These are to add an industrial feel to the piece. Carefully cut out triangular segments leaving 'spokes' behind. Children may need help with this part. Attach the cogs to the back, side or front of the factory using a butterfly pin.

5. To create child workers, lightly smudge charcoal over white paper or flexible card. Draw one or two figures at a time and cut around them, leaving a flap edge. Bend the flap and glue them inside the factory at intervals.

6. Lastly, create a lattice window frame using strips of black sugar paper glued together with PVA. Once dry, place them over the open frontage and glue them into position, using masking tape to secure them until dry. Pull the two sides together to form the boxed enclosure.

Resources
- Card, about 80 cm × 30 cm
- Brick prints
- Scissors
- Brown paint in different shades, and brushes
- PVA glue
- Black or silver paint and brushes
- Small paper plates
- Butterfly pins
- Charcoal
- White paper or flexible card
- Black sugar paper
- Masking tape

Cross-curricular links

History: investigate what life was like for working children in Victorian Britain.

Literacy: write a story about an emergency at a factory during Victorian times.

Victorian factory looms

The Industrial Revolution saw a huge increase in products being made and exported by Britain. Many factories were built and jobs became mechanised. Children were smaller in size and cheap to employ, so they were made to work in the textile industry with looms that wove all kinds of fabric. This project is stylised and graphic and includes dressing up and role-play.

Building Britain

3D, weaving and role-play

Approach

1. To prepare for weaving, neatly cut lots of strips of paper in three similar muted colours.

2. Place a sheet of black paper horizontally and with the glue stick rub a line across the top. Stick lengths of strips vertically to the glue strip. Leaving a 2 cm column on the left and a small space between each strip. Try to keep each strip straight as you work across.

3. To start weaving, rub some glue on the left side of the sheet and attach a strip horizontally. Feed it through the vertical strips, weaving under and over until you reach the right side, again keeping the strips straight. Repeat until the sheet is full. Glue any loose ends. If you like, trim the black paper to remove any ends.

4. Encourage children to wear Victorian-style clothes and pose while role-playing 'working' a loom in a factory. Take photographs, then print and enlarge them on a photocopier. Cut out the figures and stick them onto the weaving sheet.

Resources
- Scissors
- A4–A3 paper in muted colours
- A3 black sugar paper
- Glue sticks
- Digital cameras
- Photocopier
- Prints

Cross-curricular links

History: investigate the Industrial Revolution.

Literacy: read stories of children in Victorian England and write about a typical day in the life of two children; one rich, one poor.

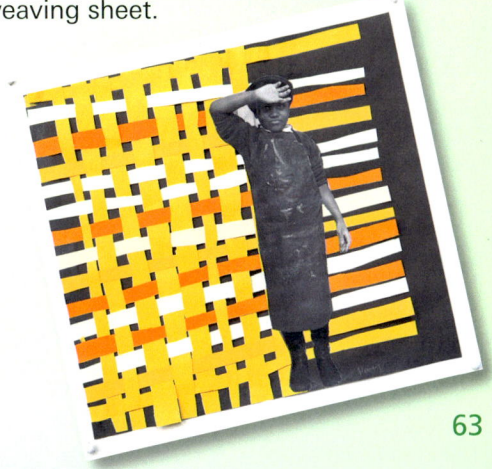

63

The Blitz: sheltering underground

During the Second World War, London was bombed nightly by the German air force. These attacks were known as the Blitz, and Londoners were forced to leave their beds night after night to take shelter, often in the tunnels of the London Underground. Sculptor Sir Henry Moore was one of those sheltering and he made studies of the people around him. This series of drawings later influenced his large-scale figurative sculptures. He captures the claustrophobia many people must have felt at the time. Photographs from the period, of people sleeping in hammocks and under blankets on the platforms and on the tracks also show this.

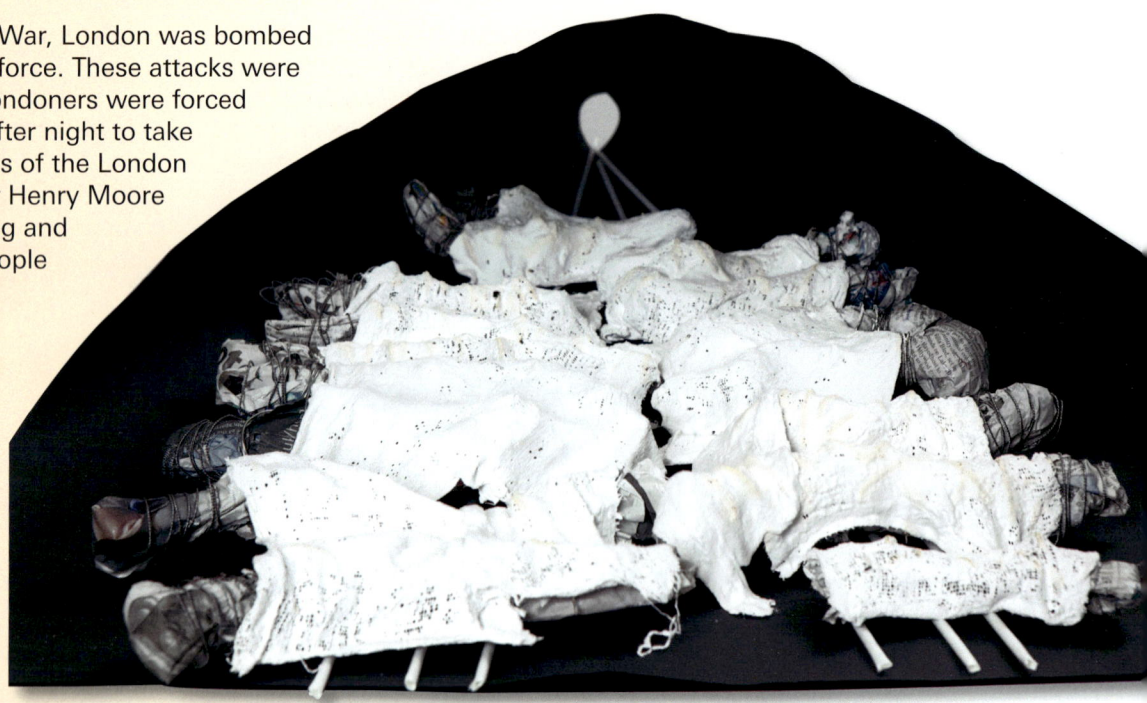

Wire and Modroc scene

Approach

1. Wrap and twist together a few sheets of newspaper.

2. Coil and bend fine modelling wire around the newspaper from top to bottom. To shape the head, fix the wire more tightly to give definition to the neck area. Once covered, bend the figure at the knee into a sleeping position. Repeat to produce another figure.

3. Lay the two figures slightly apart, on a plastic tray or on a piece of card.

4. Use one strip of Modroc that is long enough to cover both figures. Dip it into water and loosely drape it over the figures, smoothing gently by hand. When the Modroc dries, it will hold the whole piece in position.

5. To make the underground tunnel, curve a large sheet of black paper or black flexible card into a cone shape and secure with paper clips or masking tape. Paint or use art straws or masking tape for the train tracks.

Resources
- Sheets of newspaper, in 20 cm lengths
- Fine modelling wire
- Plastic tray or card base
- Modroc
- Water
- Black sugar paper or black flexible card
- Paper clips or masking tape
- Paint and brushes or paper art straws

Cross-curricular links

Design and Technology: build your own Anderson air-raid shelter.

Literacy: write a journal of a child evacuated from London during the Blitz.

Building Britain

The Blitz: a city in ruins

Iconic photographs of Britain's major cities during the Blitz show buildings turned to rubble, cinders glowing and smoke rising. One of the most famous pictures shows St. Paul's Cathedral rising above the destruction. Photos of families on the move, air-raid wardens putting out fires and looking for the injured amongst the rubble are equally dramatic. This project is a small pop-up cityscape that illustrates an explosive night-time scene from the Blitz during the Second World War.

Pop-up art

Approach

1. Fold a piece of A4 card in half. On a plastic tray or sheet, squeeze a little of each colour paint and swirl together without mixing the colours completely. Open the folded card and press one half into the paint to create a fire-lit sky.

2. Cut out a city skyline from a piece of black sugar paper. Children can add famous buildings like St. Paul's Cathedral, if they like. Stick them onto the card using the glue stick, over the lower half of the fire-lit sky and partially over the white half. Use newspaper to add details to the city skyline such as windows.

3. Fold the card in two again in the same place and make two small cuts through the fold line, 2 cm apart. Open the card and push the section forwards to make a pop-up building. Repeat two or three times to create more pop-up buildings.

4. Cut out small bomber planes and bombs and stick them onto the night sky or in front of buildings. Cut strips of newspaper and glue them onto the white section below to form streets. Add pieces of bright orange paper for explosions.

Resources
- A4 white card
- Plastic tray or sheet
- Red, orange, yellow, pink poster paints (fluorescents if possible)
- Black sugar paper
- Glue sticks
- Newspaper
- Scissors
- Bright orange paper

Cross-curricular links

History: research life in Britain during the Second World War.

Literacy: write a drama about a group of children discovering an unexploded bomb.

Science: research the conditions that allow the process of combustion.

Getting from A to B

Brunel's bridges

This project celebrates the work of the Victorian engineer, Isambard Kingdom Brunel, who built the first under-river tunnel, and many bridges, steamships and dockyards throughout Britain. He was a significant figure in the Industrial Revolution, which was a period of great change. This project gives children the opportunity to become engineers themselves. The work in these photographs was drawn from images of the Bristol Suspension Bridge and the Royal Albert Bridge in Plymouth and the class was given the brief that their bridge must hold traffic, reach either side of the river bank and have supporting towers on both sides.

3D collages

Approach

1. Choose a light shade of blue paper, tear the edges to size, and stick them on the top half of a piece of cartridge paper. Do the same with a darker shade of blue and stick it on the bottom half of the paper. This will form the river. For the river banks, add torn pieces of green paper to the side of the picture. Avoid leaving any white spaces.

2. Apply glue to the collage and using the white art straws, cut and bend pieces to form the bridge. To avoid sticky fingers place each straw carefully in position rather than applying glue to each straw.

3. Look at steamships of the period and draw small silhouette versions. Glue onto the river.

Resources
- Blue and green paper in different shades
- PVA glue
- A3 cartridge paper
- White paper art straws

Cross-curricular links

History: research the great engineering advances of Victorian times.
Literacy: write an account of a sailor on the first steamship ever built.

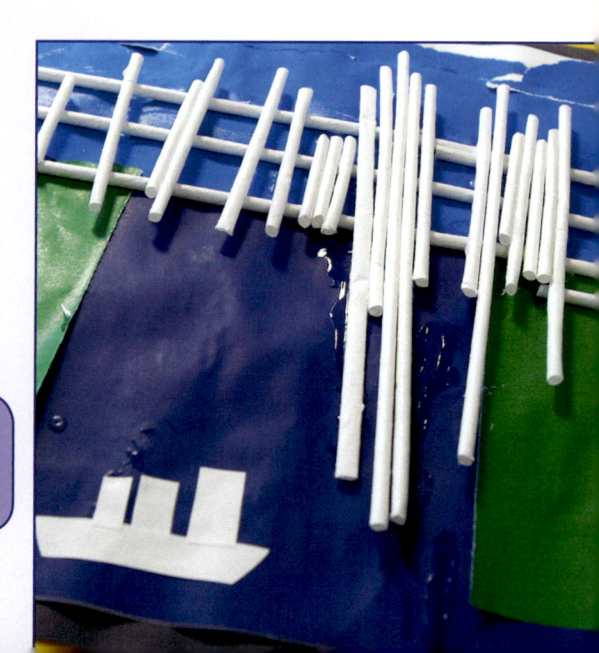

Getting from A to B

Bridges for this millennium

Modern bridge design is often as sleek and stylish as any piece of contemporary art. But a bridge has a job to do. Show children a vibrant collection of images of futuristic bridges and encourage them to try their hand at being designers.

Maquette-making

Approach

1. Explain to children how to make a maquette, or small-scale model of a sculpture or architectural work. A maquette is used to visualise and test shapes and ideas. Show images from the internet of modern bridges, explaining some of the design problems.

2. Give children A4 and A3 paper, scissors, glue sticks and an A4 sheet of coloured card as a base. Ask them to find different ways to use rectangular strips of paper to make 3D shapes. Discuss the difference between 2D, or flat shapes, which have height and width, and 3D shapes, which have height, width and depth. Suggest bending, folding, pleating, rolling and twisting. Children can come up with many other ideas.

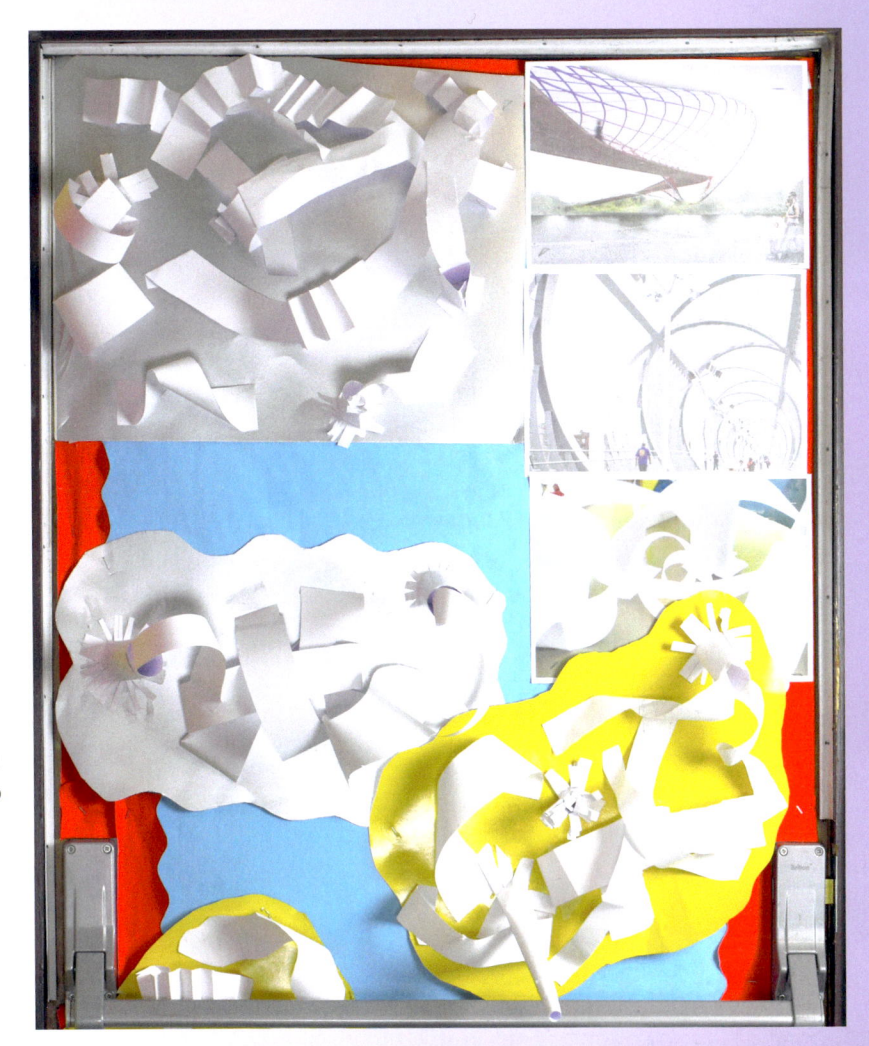

3. Discuss how the images of bridges on the internet were photographed. Give groups a camera and ask them to take close-up photographs looking through their experimental maquettes. Look at the results and encourage children to discuss them.

4. Working in groups, use the paper maquettes as a basis to make new maquettes made of card. Ask children to design an imaginative bridge structure. Have them think about who would use the bridge and what they need to do to build the bridge. Photograph the results.

Resources
- A4 and A3 paper
- Scissors
- Glue sticks
- A4 coloured card
- Internet images of modern bridges
- Cameras

Cross-curricular links

Science: examine the forces that a bridge needs to withstand. Investigate using different materials and shapes to build model bridges. Which will hold the most toy cars?

Roman arches

Start by looking at pictures of bridges built by the Romans. The arch was invented by the Romans and is one of the strongest load-bearing structures we know. Arches can even be constructed without the blocks that form the arch being cemented together, as each piece supports the other.

Resources
- Pipe cleaners
- Lolly sticks
- PVA glue
- Foil
- Paper art straws or metallic paper
- Plastic buttons
- Drawing pencils
- Red felt, fabric or paper
- Plastic trays
- Air-drying clay
- Water
- Modelling tools
- Ochre poster paint and brushes
- A4 cardboard

Construct an arch

Approach

1. To make Roman soldiers, wrap a pipe cleaner around a lolly stick and glue to form arms. For armour, roll foil around the stick and arms.
2. To create a weapon, use paper art straws or a rolled piece of foil and attach to an arm.
3. For a shield, poke a button onto the other arm through the holes.
4. Use a drawing pencil to add a fierce face, gluing it at the top of the lolly stick. Add a shiny metal helmet with a red crest using foil and red paper. For the cape, cut a rectangle of red felt, fabric or paper and glue the two top corners together at the neck.
5. To make a bridge, work clay into individual blocks on a plastic tray and use these to make and join two pillars in an arch. Join each block securely (cross-hatch the adjoining surfaces, add a little water, push together and smooth with a tool). See if you can make a keystone – the triangular-shaped block in the middle that holds it together.
6. Push the Roman soldiers into the wet clay. Allow to dry and paint with a wash of ochre. Very carefully transfer to an A4 sheet of cardboard with a background of choice. Please note that the bricks may separate when dry.

Cross-curricular links

Design and Technology: build an arch that is strong enough to stand on.

History: research the Roman's invasion of Britain and Hadrian's Wall.

Literacy: describe a young Roman's experience on Hadrian's Wall, far from home.

Science: research the arch in nature.

Getting from A to B

Arches in viaducts

During the Industrial Revolution, the viaduct played an important role, allowing the transport of all kinds of materials such as coal from the mines to the ports. In this project, children can make a mono print of a viaduct.

Mono printing

Approach

1. Before showing a presentation about viaducts, ask children to focus on looking for outline shapes: rectangles, circles, arches. Hand out A3 paper and marker pens for recording ideas. Discuss their recorded ideas and ask them to select their favourite shapes or parts. They should simplify and enlarge these to an A4 design in preparation for making a mono print. Photocopy the designs to add colour with ink or paint later.

2. Make a mono print using a roller to spread a thin layer of printing ink all over an inking plate. Next, place a sheet of paper on top of the inking plate and use a pencil to draw a design on the paper. Pressing hard with the pencil will result in a clearer print. Peel back the paper to reveal a unique mono print.

3. To add another dimension to the print, use PVA glue to stick pieces of tissue paper to the paper before placing it on the plate.

4. Try different ways of making a mono print. Ink the plate as above, then draw directly into the printing ink with a cotton wool bud or narrow piece of card, removing some of the ink as you draw. Place a sheet of paper on the plate, smooth down gently and peel back the paper to reveal the print.

Resources
- Presentation about viaducts
- A3 paper
- Marker pens
- A4 paper
- Coloured drawing inks or water paints
- Paintbrushes
- Rollers
- Black printing ink
- Inking plate
- Pencils
- PVA glue and tissue paper
- Cotton wool bud or narrow piece of card

Cross-curricular links

Geography: research coal and find out where it is mined.
History: investigate the importance of coal mining.
Literacy: explain how to make a mono print.

69

Tunnel vision

Long tunnels, short tunnels, under the sea or through a mountain, there is something exciting about travelling through tunnels. In this project, children can investigate the experience of travelling through a tunnel.

Resources
- Clay cutter tools (adult use only)
- Clay guides
- Slabs of clay
- Clay modelling tools
- Newspaper sheets
- Rolling pins
- A3 tourist maps
- A3 paper
- Glue sticks or PVA glue
- Oil pastels
- A3 paper
- Laminator (if possible)
- Tape
- Model cars
- Camera

Clay modelling

Approach

1. Using the clay cutter tool, cut slabs of clay 3 cm thick. Place the clay on a stack of newspaper with a pair of clay guides on either side. Roll out the clay with the rolling pin. Remove the guides, turn the paper stack around and continue rolling the clay until it is a rectangular shape. Lift the clay rectangles off the newspaper and place over rolling pins. Children can now create brick patterns on the clay with clay tools. The clay tunnels will take several days to dry, resting over the rolling pins (which act as moulds).

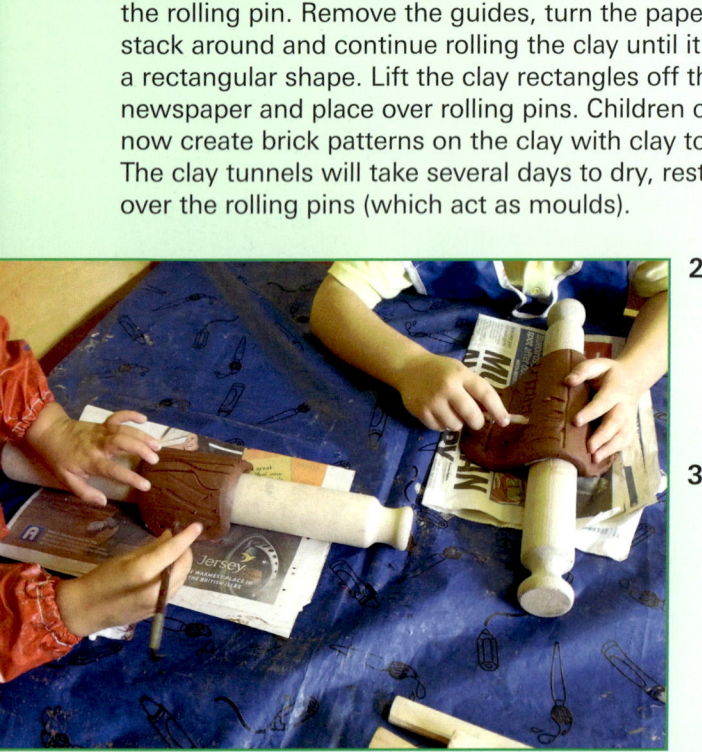

2. Show children maps from the local tourist office. Discuss what the colours represent, for example, *what colour are the roads?* Hand out A3 paper, glue and torn pieces of maps. Show children how to glue a piece of map onto A3 paper. Draw details in oil pastels, for example, a road to extend from the map onto the paper.

3. Laminate the maps if possible. Tape a collection of children's completed 'maps' together and let them arrange them where they want to place their tunnels. Use model cars to test-drive the tunnels and take photos while looking through the 'tunnel vision'.

Cross-curricular links

Geography: invent a new country and make a map with a key.
Science: investigate the building of a major underground tunnel, for example, the Channel Tunnel.

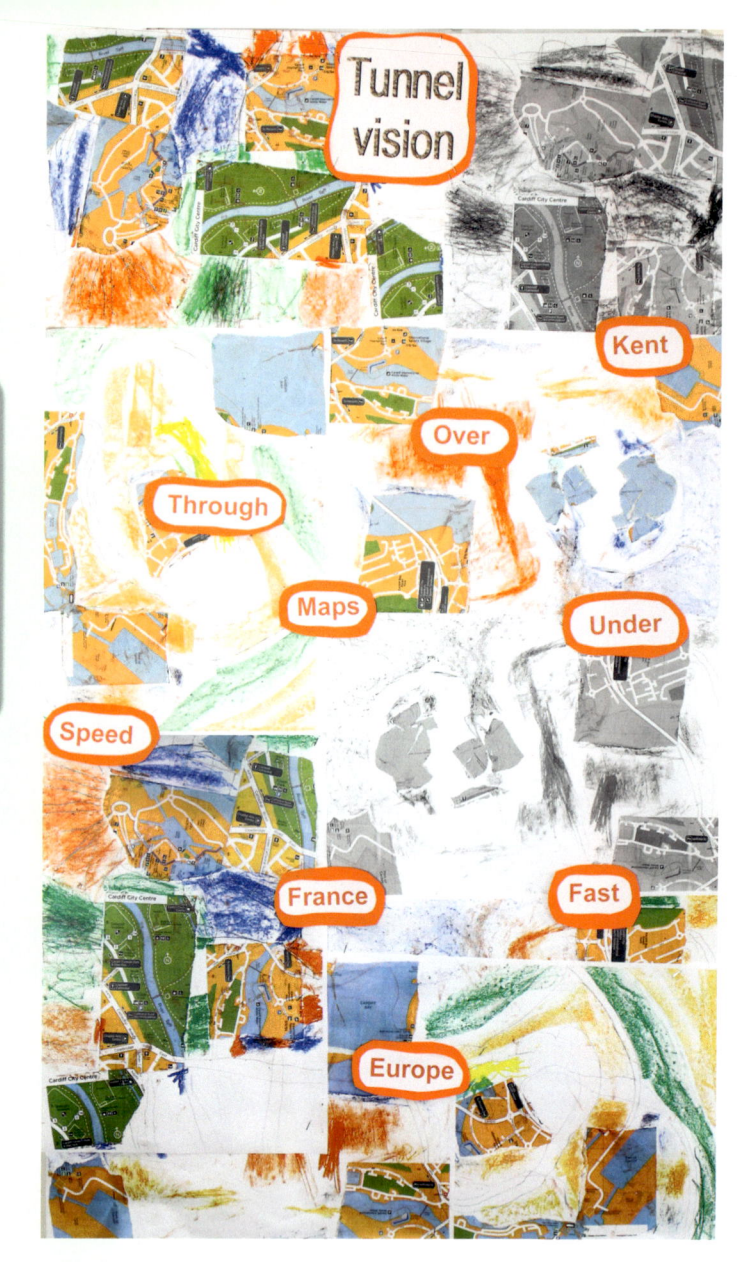

A panorama of our school

Show children their own street or school on the internet. Through observation, drawings and photographs, this project aims to show children how to create their own mini panoramas of their environment.

Creating mini panoramas

Approach

1. Talk about outline shapes. If children think of mathematical shapes, link the shapes they know with different things they can see in the classroom. For example, use an object such as a bottle or key and demonstrate how to draw an outline shape.

2. Take children into the playground with A4 paper, clipboards, marker pens and cameras. Encourage them to look for and collect outline shapes by drawing what they see and taking photographs, for example, trees, goal posts, playground furniture. Remind them how to use a camera and explain that they should photograph shapes, not whole landscapes.

3. Download children's photographs. Talk about them and select some for photocopying. Children can work in groups and pool their drawings and photographs together. Each group will need glue sticks, scissors, half of an A3 sheet of cartridge paper and oil pastels to add colour. Show them how to tear and cut out their outline drawings and photographs. Also demonstrate how to arrange them along the cartridge paper strip. Encourage children to add extra detail and colour, before sticking their pieces in place using a glue stick.

4. They should add a watery wash of coloured ink to their background and trim any excess paper, before folding back a strip of paper to make the picture stand up.

5. Display the children's panoramas.

Getting from A to B

Resources
- Internet access to show the school location on Google Earth
- A4 paper and clipboards
- Marker pens
- Cameras
- Glue sticks
- Scissors
- A3 cartridge paper divided in half
- Oil pastels
- Water and coloured drawing inks and brushes

Cross-curricular links

Geography: find a city in each continent of the world using maps on the internet.
History: discuss how people communicated before the internet and mobile phones.
Literacy: write about a trip to somewhere in the world.
Maths: list all the familiar shapes and think about ways in which they are used in real life.

Visiting heritage houses

All over the United Kingdom famous houses can be found that are part of Britain's architectural heritage. This project involves a class visit to a heritage house. In these photographs for the project, children visited 17th century Tredegar House in South Wales, which provided the inspiration for designing wallpaper and fabric.

Resources
- Clipboards
- A4 paper
- Marker pens
- A1 paper
- Oil pastels and chalk pastels
- Textiles
- Plastic tablecloths
- Dye sticks
- Fabric
- Fabric paints
- Non-spill paint pots, water and brushes

Designing wallpaper and fabric

Approach

1. With children, visit a famous local mansion. Afterwards, talk about what they enjoyed during the visit. Suggest recreating some of these things, such as curtains and wallpaper.

2. Have children work outside with clipboards and A4 paper, looking for and collecting the shapes of leaves and flowers using marker pens. Back in the classroom, encourage children to share their drawings. Ask each child to choose one to enlarge and use to fill an A4 sheet.

3. To make wallpaper, get children to work in groups with marker pens on A1 paper, drawing their enlarged designs. When children have made the first drawing, ask them to turn the paper around, to make a different design in a different space. Encourage them to add colour with oil pastels and colour in the background with chalk pastels – a different colour for each group.

4. Use plastic tablecloths to protect the work surfaces. Demonstrate how to use fabric paints. Working in groups as they did for the wallpaper activity, ask each child to draw their own leaf or flower shapes with dye sticks onto the fabric and then use fabric paints to fill them in. Display as curtains for the home corner of the classroom.

Cross-curricular links

History: research local mansions and their interior decorations. In what period were the mansions built? Which designs were popular?

Literacy: write a story about growing up in a mansion.

Science: explain why plants and trees have leaves.